HDQ

:es
Medford, U..

DATE DUE			7/01
SEP 4 01			
FEB 01 02			
4/15			
5/8			
5/27			
GAYLORD			PRINTED IN U.S.A.

Selected
Architecture
Public Buildings - Private Residences

Whitney
JACKSON COUNTY LIBRARY SERVICES
MEDFORD, OREGON 97501

Selected
Architecture

Public Buildings - Private Residences

AUTHOR Francisco Asensio Cerver

EDITORIAL DIRECTOR Paco Asensio

PROJECT COORDINATOR Ivan Bercedo, architect

DESIGN Mireia Casanovas Soley

LAYOUT Òscar Lleonart Ruiz

TEXT

IVAN BERCEDO Introduction, Guggenheim Museum,
High Speed Station in Lyon-Satôlas Airport,
Le Sémaphore, DRTE Arles, Tobu Golf Club, Faculty of Journalism,
The Box, Männistön Church and Parish Center, Villa Wilbrink,
Villa M, Stein Residence, The Flower House, Barnes House,
Type/Variant House, Collective Housing for the Cheesecake Consortium,
House in Tateshina.

CAYETANO CARDELÚS Central Beheer.

RAMON ESTEVE House at Na Xemena.

FINN KAPPE Kappe Tamuri Residence.

JORGE MESTRE European Court of Human Rights,
The Holz Altenried Exhibition Hall and Warehouse, Kol Ami Temple, Linear House.

MAURICI PLA Palafolls Sports Pavilion, Kaze-no-Oka Crematorium.

MOISÉS PUENTE Faculty of Economics .

ITZIAR SEN Arken Museum of Modern Art, Capistrano Beach House.

PROOFREADING Amber Ockrassa

© 1998 Francisco Asensio Cerver

Published by
Whitney Library of Design
An imprint of Watson & Guptill Publications
New York

ISBN: 0-8230-4780-6

Printed in Spain

No part of this publication may be reproduced, stored in retrieval system or transmitted in any form or by means, electronic, mechanical, photocopying, recording or otherwise, without the prior written permission of the owner of the copyright.

Public Buildings

Private Residences

These days there are no dominant guidelines which mark out a direction for architects to follow, or even set trends to get around stylistic doubts. Rather than being a formal question, this situation means the absence of dogmas and admits a wide range of criteria.

As opposed to the manifestos or given patterns of other times, the present-day trend of architecture publications is to present projects individually and evaluate each of them independently. There is no need to try and draw a common conclusion. There is no point in sacrificing the wealth of a kaleidoscopic viewpoint to the desire to come up with an all-embracing idea.

In a society with an extraordinary capacity for disseminating images, any attempt to establish orders or written laws of aesthetics is pointless. A photographic reportage will reach further afield than any rule book.

The buildings shown on the following pages are each presented independently. The images and graphic documentation are accompanied by a text which analyses the history of the commission, specific characteristics of site and program, the ideas lying behind the project and the technical solutions used. It is in this particular world that we have to seek the reason for the form which is ultimately adopted.

This leads us to an architecture in which the particular and the specific are first and foremost. It is not just the general concept that matters, but also the treatment of the materials and the attention to detail: it is only when we look into the particularities of the project that the chosen solutions and the ultimate form of the building make sense. While the image is the principal vehicle of information, if it is not backed up by anything more substantial, it can only ever be banal. Form stands at the end of the itinerary, which means that to reveal its mysteries we have to go back to the creative process.

For us, public buildings and private residences are two quite distinct fields for the architect. There are very basic differences between them: in the case of public architecture the user has no specific profile, whereas every decision must be adapted to the tastes and habits of the client. Likewise, dimensions, the type of furnishing and activities which are carried on in public spaces are very different to those of the domestic sphere. For all of these reasons, we have divided this book into two corresponding chapters.

Public buildings

Despite the differences in size, budget, program, appearance, effects on the surroundings and so for of the projects we present in this volume, there is one quality which is common to all of them: they are public buildings.

The public building is granted a degree of license which sets it apart from private architecture. Behind each is an identifiable developer, be it the government or a company, yet they are on show to the eyes of the unknown visitor. No one person can feel themself to be entirely their owner (even if they are, to all effects and purposes), as they are buildings which are intended to be used by others, and visited only occasionally by the legal owner.

In this sense, if the life cycle of a house is much longer (perhaps an entire lifetime, or even that of several generations of one family), in the public sector the importance of immediate perception comes to the fore.

This does not imply that as a spectacular form of architecture it is necessarily less subtle; rather it means that the chance to produce emotions is transferred to other areas such as the relationship with the city, internal itineraries that are a continuation of streets or the possibility of creating a parenthesis in the continual traffic of urban life.

Guggenheim Museum

Frank O. Gehry

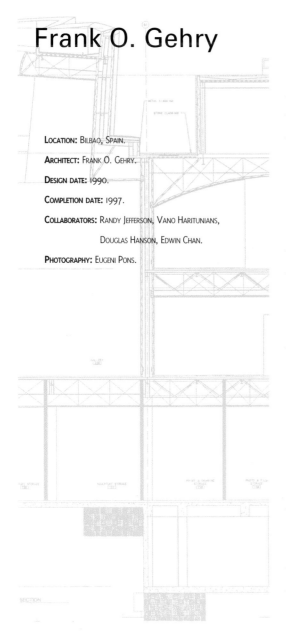

LOCATION: BILBAO, SPAIN.

ARCHITECT: FRANK O. GEHRY.

DESIGN DATE: 1990.

COMPLETION DATE: 1997.

COLLABORATORS: RANDY JEFFERSON, VANO HARITUNIANS,

DOUGLAS HANSON, EDWIN CHAN.

PHOTOGRAPHY: EUGENI PONS.

Bilbao is an industrial city with an important history in metallurgy. The city is divided by the Nervión River, whose banks are lined with steel mills, blast furnaces, shipyards, gigantic cranes, and warehouses. This panorama has formed an integral part of Bilbao´s image since the industrial revolution. It is a harsh landscape, but also one of great visual impact and profound force.

Industrial reconversion has meant that many of these complexes have become obsolete, and they now stand idle and abandoned. Several years ago, therefore, the Basque regional government came up with a plan to revitalize the river area and renovate and convert these factory buildings, substituting their original industrial activities with commercial, financial, and service sector uses.

The Basque authorities have tried to boost this initiative by commissioning several major projects, many on the banks of the Nervión. Among the most important of these are the metro, designed by Norman Foster, the new airport terminal by Santiago Calatrava, the Palacio de Congresos y de la Música (Convention Center and Concert Hall) by Federico Soriano, a plan for the reorganization of the Ibano-Ibarra area by César Pelli, a train-and-bus station by Michael Wildford, and the Guggenheim Museum itself.

In a restricted competition, Gehry's project was selected over projects presented by Arata Isozaki and Coop Himmelblau. Both the Basque authorities and the representatives from the Guggenheim Foundation were looking for a unique and iconoclastic building which would cause as great an impact as Frank Lloyd Wright' s building for the Guggenheim Museum' s headquarters in New York, and at the same time would attract international attention in the art world and become a symbol of the city. In a certain sense, the building was not

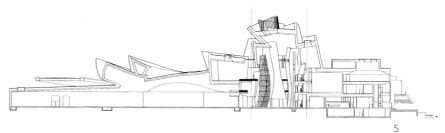

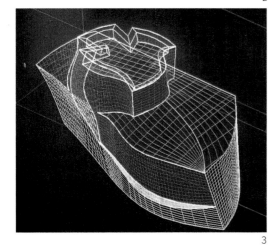

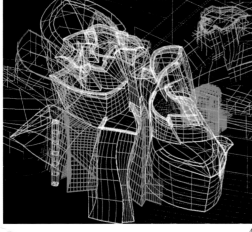

1. Nighttime view of the estuary in Bilbao.

2. Other large-scale facilities such as the Congress Center are being built in the environs of the museum.

3, 4. Computer-assisted design plays a very important role in defining the final project.

5. Section of the atrium.

6. The curved volumes are clad with titanium, whereas the rest of the walls are covered with limestone.

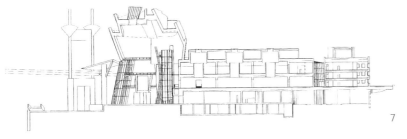

7

only commissioned for its cultural end, but also as a symbol of the enormous metamorphosis which Bilbao is undergoing.

The museum is located on the riverbanks next to a busy suspension bridge, which Gehry took into account from the very beginning as forming part of the project. A great number of comparisons and similes can be made, but according to the architect himself, the work is based on the following themes: the film 'metropolis', by Fritz Lang, the sculptures of Brancusi, the image of a quarry, and above all, the vigor and controlled force which the city of Bilbao exudes.

The greatest influence on the final form that the building has taken, though, is of course Gehry's own style, his way of working from free sketches and models which are transferred almost literally to the computer screen, where they are mathematically analyzed in order to resolve technical and structural aspects. Thus, the museum carries the mark of Gehry above all.

The museum is composed of a large central atrium, 50 meters high (1.5 times that of the New York Guggenheim) and crowned by a "metal flower", and three wings going off to the east, the south and the west. To the north lies the river, where what would have been the fourth wing gives way to a large glass entrance.

Each of the three wings is designed to contain different types of exhibits. The permanent collection is located in the south wing, in a series of consecutive square exhibition halls. The west wing houses the collection of contemporary art, distributed in seven halls of unique and varied shapes. Temporary exhibits will be shown in a large hall (130 by 30m) which extends sinuously towards the east.

The auditorium, as well as the restaurant and shops, are on the ground floor and are accessible from the plaza at the front of the museum. They have their own entrance and can therefore function independently from the museum. All the auxiliary service departments are located in the basement, which is accessed from a service road.

13

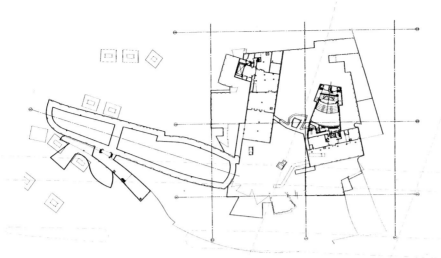

9. Basement floor.

10. First floor.

11. Second floor.

9

14

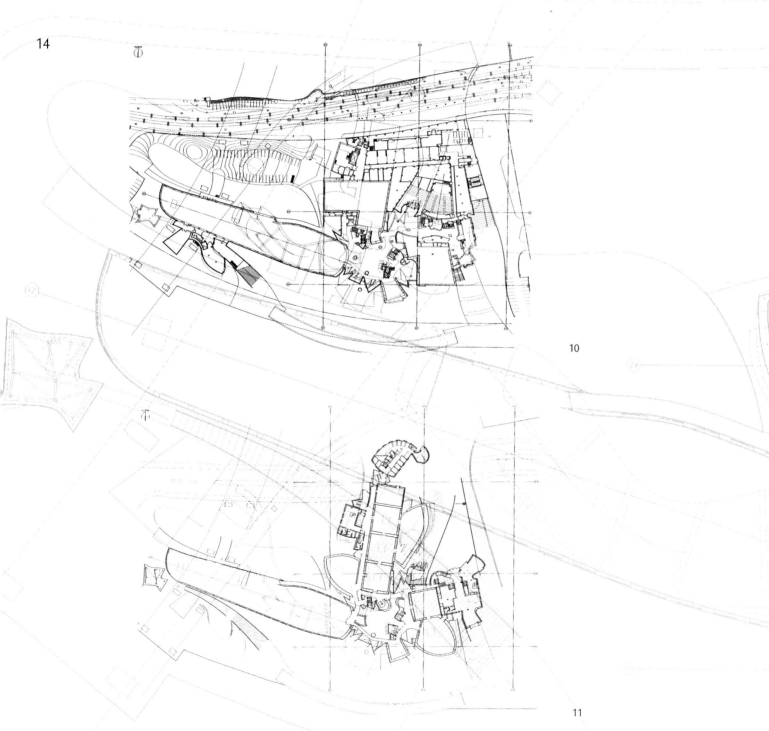

10

11

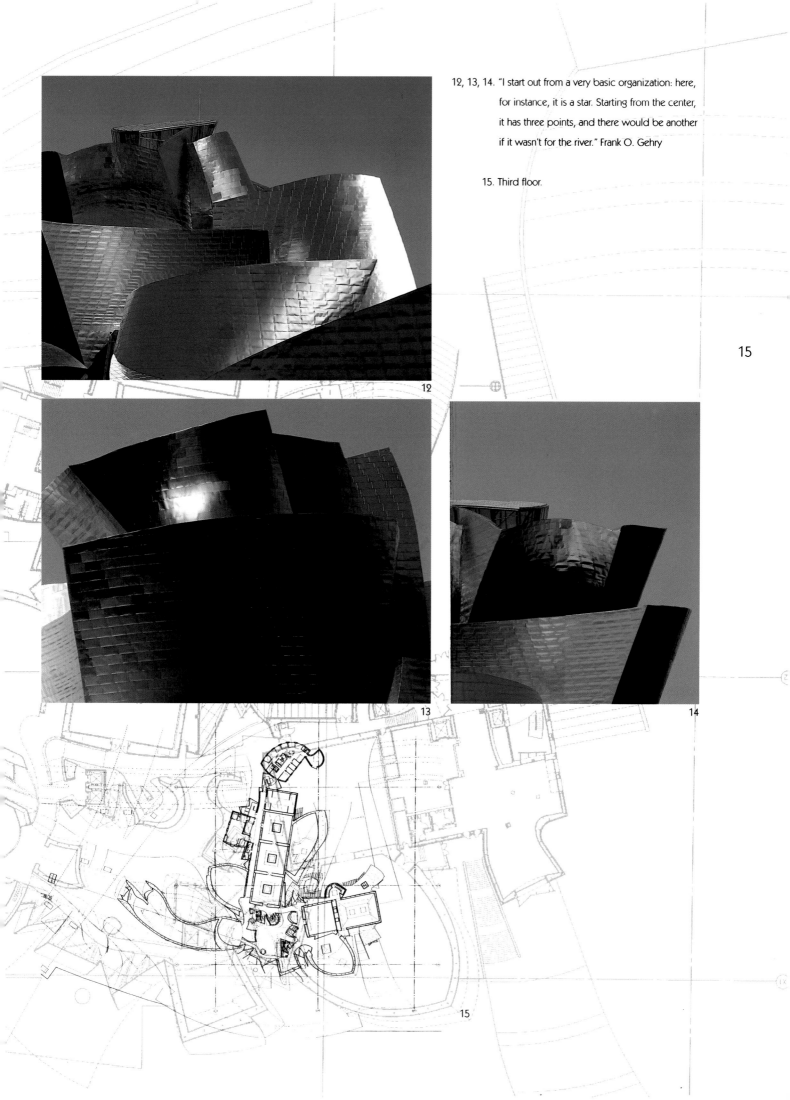

12, 13, 14. "I start out from a very basic organization: here, for instance, it is a star. Starting from the center, it has three points, and there would be another if it wasn't for the river." Frank O. Gehry

15. Third floor.

15

12

13

14

15

16. "In my projects, including this one, when we take the first steps there are no sculptural aspects as such; we see a series of colored wooden blocks which represent the building's functions; in this case, a museum. And these blocks, with no sculptural form, join up like pieces of a puzzle. As the project advances, we work on the technical aspect."

17, 18. According to the architect, the forms of this museum are inspired by scenes from the film Metropolis by Fritz Lang.

19. Transversal section.

17

18

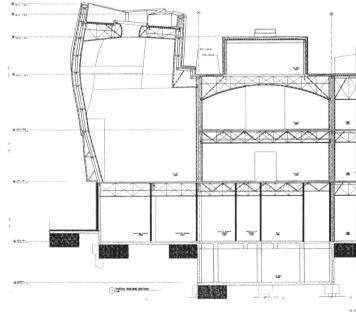

19

European Court of Human Rights

Richard Rogers

LOCATION: STRASBOURG, FRANCE..

COMPLETION DATE: DECEMBER OF 1995.

COST: 455,000,000 FrF.

CLIENT: CONSEIL DE L'EUROPE.

ARCHITECTS: SIR RICHARD ROGERS (ROGERS PARTNERSHIP LDT.),
CLAUDE BUCHER.

COLLABORATORS: LAURIE ABBOT, PETER ANGRAVE, EIKE BECKER,
MIKE DAVIES, ELLIOT BOYD, KARIN EGGE,
MARCO GOLDSCHMIED, PASCALE GIBON, LENNART GRUT,
IVAN HARBOUR, AMARJIT KALSI, SZE-KING KAN,
CARMEL LEWIN, AVTAR LOTAY, JOHN LOWE,
LOUISE PALOMBA, KIM QUAZI, PASCALE ROUSSEAU,
YUU TOH, SARAH TWEEDIE, ANDREW TYLEY,
YOSHIYUKI UCHIYAMA, JOHN YOUNG
(RICHARD ROGERS PARTNERSHIP), OVE ARUP,
OMINIUM TECHNIQUE EUROPEÉN (STRUCTURAL AND
SERVICES ENGINEERS), THORNE WHEATLEY ASSOCIATES
(QUANTITY SURVEYORS), DAVID JARVIS ASSOCIATES,
DAN KILEY (LANDSCAPE CONSULTANTS), LIGHTING DESIGN
PARTNERSHIP (LIGHTING CONSULTANTS), SOUND RESEARCH
LABORATORIES, COMMINS INGEMANSSON
(ACOUSTIC CONSULTANTS).

PHOTOGRAPHS: F. BUSAM/ARCHITEKTURPHOTO.

The Court of Human Rights is the result of a 1989 tender to provide the Council of Europe with a new building to meet the needs arising from changes that were occurring within the institution at that time.

The architect's aim was to create a design that would be a symbolic and programmatic representation of the work carried out by the Court of Human Rights; an open and transparent building expressing a desire for transparency in justice. A democracy does not conceal its machinery, it does not hide secrets behind thick, dark, heavy walls. Everything is open to the public, everything is done in the light, open to the gaze of anyone who wishes to watch, since there is nothing to hide.

The project seems to have taken its form from an organism; it has a certain animal air. One reading proposed by Richard Rogers is that one could say that "it is a jointed ensemble of head and body". The two components are connected by way of the vertical communications. In this reading, the head is the public section where the rooms of the Court and the Commission are located, and the body or tail houses the administrative section.

The head is dramatic and expressive. The steel and glass facade absorbs and reflects its surroundings, sunlight, shadows, rain and wind. Two metallic cylinders, each supported by a group of three pillars, appear to float at a certain distance from the ground. A third cylinder, situated on a lower level and made of glass, houses the entrance and links the other two. The entrance is reached either by climbing an exterior flight of stairs or by walking up a long, twisting ramp, which affords the visitor a lengthy, preliminary view of the building. It is a progressive, although frontal, approach to the symmetrical image created by the juxtaposition of the two cylinders.

The character of the body is quite different. In fact, the dialectic rela-

1

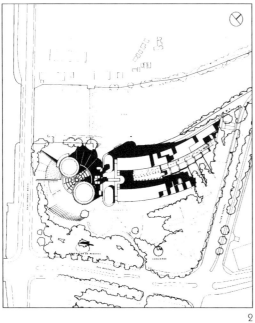

2

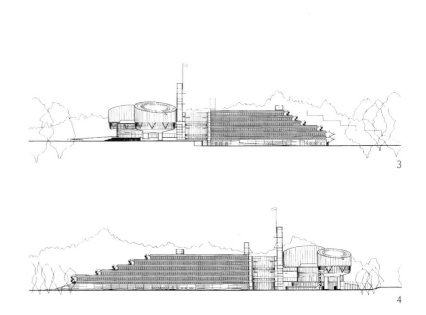

3

4

5

6

1. View of the entrance.

2. Site plan.

3. East elevation.

4. West elevation.

5. Rogers' architecture combines high technology with respect for the environment. The landscape project was directed by Dan Kiley.

6. Detail of the inner court between the two phalanxes of offices.

7. Section of the assembly halls.

7

tionship between these two parts is a key element in the design. In contrast with the head, the body is serene; two curved wings encircling an elongated courtyard featuring a stepped sheet of water. The water is in constant motion, descending from one plane to the next all the way to the end of the building. Vegetation extends along both sides of the façade. The two wings slope gently groundwards. They are stepped like the sheet of water, and finally bury themselves in the landscape.

The building comprises 28,000 m^2 total floor space, of which 860 m^2 correspond to the courtroom (47 fixed seats and 52 additional ones), 520 m^2 to the Commission Room (41 + 30 seats), 4,500 m^2 to auxiliary meeting rooms, and 16,500 m^2 to offices.

As in almost all of Richard Roger's buildings, the attention paid to detail is astonishing. His architecture always displays a desire for transparency and lightness. The dimensions of the structural elements are minimal. To achieve this the loads are divided in different directions, and are distributed between supports and stays. Rather than trying to conceal the structure, Rogers glorifies it by using high technology.

This preoccupation with technical solutions is widespread among British architects who undertake large commissions: Norman Foster, Nicholas Grimshaw, Alsop & Störmer, Michael Hopkins, Ian Ritchie, Future Systems etc. This phenomenon bears witness to the British industrial heritage in steel dating from the nineteenth century. However, it is also due in large part to the quality work of some British construction engineering offices, such as Ove Arup and Peter Rice, and their close collaboration with most of the architects mentioned.

8. Overview of the foyer.

9, 10, 11. One of the most important facets of Rogers' work is the design of the vertical communication elements. If we look back at some of the most significant buildings in his career (the Pompidou Centre in Paris, or the Lloyd's building in London), we see how stairways and lifts are the protagonists of space.

8

9

10

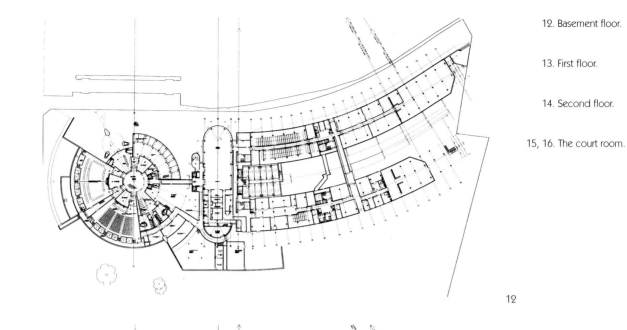

12. Basement floor.

13. First floor.

14. Second floor.

15, 16. The court room.

12

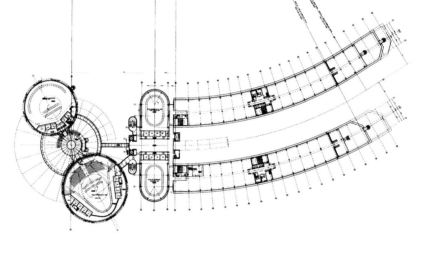

13

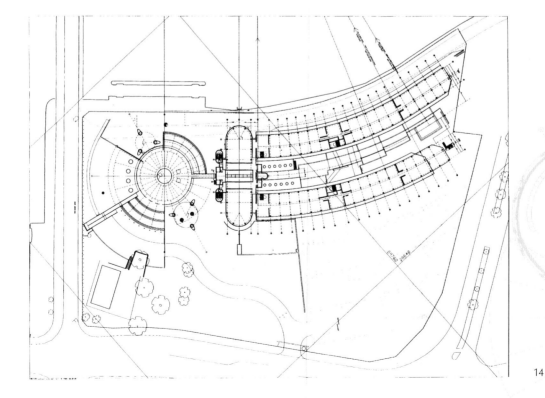

14

15

16

High Speed Station in Lyon-Satôlas Airport

Santiago Calatrava

LOCATION: LYON, FRANCE.

DATE OF CONSTRUCTION: 1996.

PROMOTER: THE CHAMBER OF COMMERCE AND
INDUSTRY OF LYON AND SNCF.

ARCHITECT: SANTIAGO CALATRAVA I VALLS.

COLLABORATORS: ALEXIS BURRET, SEBASTIEN MÉRNET
(THEAD ARCHITECTS), DAVID LONG,
L. BURR (ASSISTANTS).

PHOTOGRAPHS: RALPH RICHTER / ARCHITEKTURPHOTO.

Santiago Calatrava has the singular capacity to convey via shape the forces trapped in the building elements themselves. He manages to intuitively express the tensions that converge in the static and thus unfold a poetry intrinsic to the tectonic.

As a boy, Calatrava attended an old school of Arts and Professions and, even today, many years later, continues revindicating the direct learning of shapes via the drawing in those courses to carvers, engravers and glassworkers.

He preserves from that epoch, memory aside, a certain disposition: the direct linking between drawing and object, the conscientious development, almost sculptural, of the models in section, more proper to the builder of a piece or a designer of an object, than to someone who is trying to develop a program or distribute some needs. His language comes from the streamlining of the idea, almost from the plasticization of the form at the very last moment when movement was frozen.

Nevertheless, in the architecture of Calatrava, there is not only a representation of the convergent tensions, but also an exploration of the symbolic possibilities of the structures. The technical solutions adopted in his buildings, though extremely sophisticated, appear quite natural, hence, their approximation to nature, to animal skeletons, to trees. The structures are not designed as simple zoomorphic analogues, it is the end result which itself convokes logic and evokes nature.

The Lyon-Satàlas station is the first one to join an airport to a high-speed railway network in Europe. Thirty kilometers to the North of Lyon, the airport is not only attractive to the city's dwellers, but also has the same effect on visitors from other, more distant capitals like Paris and Marseilles. The authorities in the Rhône-Alps region, the Chamber of Commerce and Industry for Lyon and the national railway company, SNCF, in 1990 put out to tender for what they wanted to be the building emblematic of the transformation beginning just then in communications. The competition was won by one of the foreign architects who put in a bid,

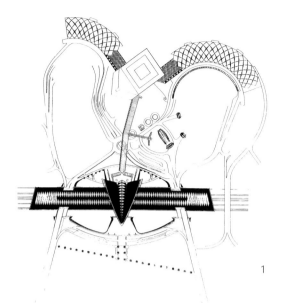

1

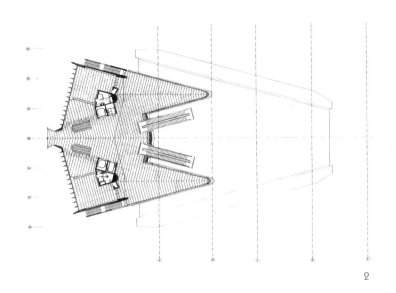

2

28

5

6

7

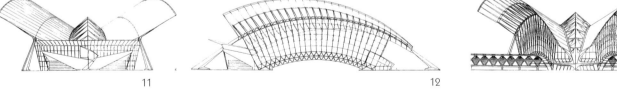

11

12

13

1. Site plan.

2. Ground plan of the footbridge.

3. Ground plan of the foyer.

4. Ground plan of the platforms.

5. Side view.

6. Detail of the intersection of the concrete and metal structures.

7. View of the pedestrian entrance.

8. Detail of the side wall of the foyer.

9. Nighttime view of the foyer.

10. Detail of one of the information desks.

11. East elevation.

12. North elevation.

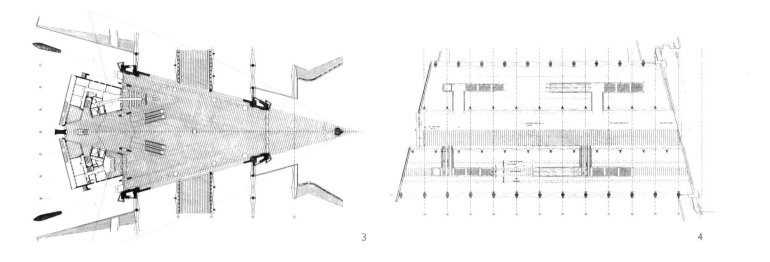

3

4

8

9

10

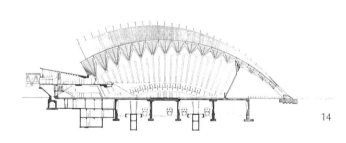

14

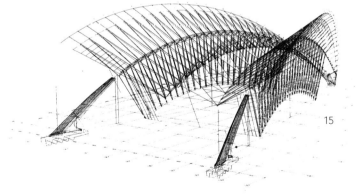

15

13. West elevation.

14. Longitudinal section.

15. Axonometric study.

16

17

18

Santiago Calatrava, who knew how to pick up the reins of tradition of the large engineering works dating from the last century, and to infuse his large infrastructure projects with a symbolic dimension.

In the Lyon-Satôlas station, Santiago Calatrava uses two preferred compositional devices; symmetry and duality. The symmetry comes from the will to simplify the floor.

His architecture is based on the constructive and hence, the essential vision of his projects is the sectional view. The floor is the order and section, the beauty. The duality or dialogue gives tension to the project, but it also gives it unity, given that the parts attain their meaning by interrelating, thereby constructing the totality.

The station covers two perpendicular movements with the different structures that highlight this crossing. A vaulted ceiling, built with an oblique network of white concrete beams and rhomboid-shaped glass skylights, covering in more than half a kilometer the six train platforms projected, allowing a scheduled extending of two tracks more for the regional connection with Lyon. The ribs of the ceiling rest on inclined pillars that bifurcate. The tracks are excavated in the ground and the vault scarcely juts out above the entrance's height. Because of the thickness of the concrete network and its markedly longitudinal character, the impression given is that of a tunnel or cavern prodigiously lit by natural light. Transversally, this ceiling is crossed above by a large triangular-shaped floor hall that connects the main entrance with: on one vertex, the unit and the taxi and bus terminals; and on the opposite side, the passenger walkway belt measuring 180m taking passengers to the airport.

The hall's ceiling is the station's emblematic element. Two gigantic steel arches resting on the vertex of the triangle situated opposite the entrance and on the two vertices of the opposite side, thus defining the North and South façades. Over them, an angular structure of steel and glass section has been built that can be turned to improve the hall's ventilation. On the Eastern side, between the walkway and the hall of the station's services, offices, tiket offices, restaurants, police posts, are located.

16. The concrete mesh covering the platforms.

17. The structure governs the form of the building.

18, 19. Like in most of Calatrava's projects, the building materials are limited to concrete, steel and glass.

Le Sémaphore

Christian Drevet

LOCATION: ROUSSILLON, FRANCE.

DATE OF CONSRUCTION: SEPTEMBRE 1994.

PROMOTER: VILLE DE ROUSILLON (ISÈRE).

COSTE: 11.185.411 F.

ARCHITECTS: CHRISTIAN DREVET ARCHITECTURES, NICOLAS GUILLOT.

COLLABORATORS: BRUNO BOSSARD, JEAN-CHRISTIAN CHEZE
(ASSISTANTS), BERNARD THAON (ACOUSTICS),
ALAIN RANVIER (METAL STRUCTURE),
GUY POULAIN (CONCRETE STRUCTURE),
JEAN-PIERRE CHAILLEUX (FLUIDS),
ROBERT BLANPAIN (ECONOMIST).

PHOTOGRAPHS: ERIC SAILLET.

Le Sémaphore is a multi-use hall designed to hold theatrical spectaculars and concerts as well as parties and banquets. This is why the shape and distribution of the spaces do not faithfully conform to the typical typology of a theatre and there are clear variations (especially in the stage and auxiliary rooms), since these spaces are used both for dining and dancing.

Le Sémaphore can be found on the outskirts of the city of Rousillon, next to the southern motorway, together with several manufacturing buildings belonging to the Rhône-Poulenc company, a sports area (a swimming pool and an indoor tennis court), and a zone where it has been decided to construct a block of dwellings with the intention of enlarging the city in this direction. It is a typical outskirts landscape—scales, uses and speed, all mixed together. An environment which is broken up into egocentric and aggressive buildings. The two highways that cross the zone possess opposing characteristics—on the motorway, the cars travel at over eighty miles an hour (the building appears as an ephemeral image on a strip of almost 200 miles), while the building constitutes the main public space on the road that joins the city to the new residential area.

As an answer to these multiple sources of interference, the projects plays with three elements—a luminous mast, a metal screen and a parallelepiped.

1

2

3

4

1, 2. Details of the entrance.

3. Structure of the metal brise-soleil.

4. Detail of the sloping volume.

5. Site plan.

6, 7, 8. Ground plans:
1. Entrance.
2. Tiered seating.
3. Stage.
4. Events hall.
5. Sets.
6. Kitchen.
7. Services.
8. Dressing rooms.
9. Technical control.
10. Boxes.
11. Meeting room.
12. Repair workshop.
13. Management.
14. Backstage.
15. Corridor.

9. Longitudinal section.

10. Cross section.

11. General view of the entrance.

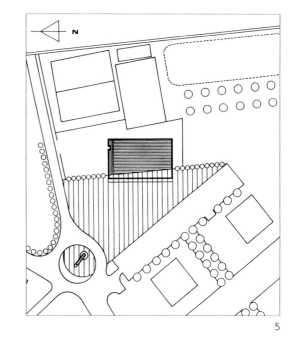

5

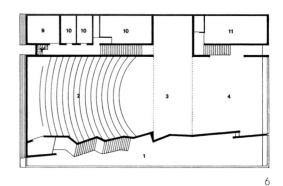

6

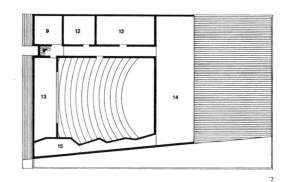

7

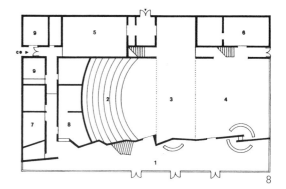

8

9

10

35

11

12

13

14

36

"Like the traffic lights in the urban storm, the 20-metre high luminous mast anchors the whole complex, it identifies it from the motorway and it inscribes itself on the collective memory. It creates a stage setting during the night like a theatre's spotlight. Like a cinema screen or a set, the metal skin protects from the east sun, defines the entrance and creates a backdrop for the perspective of the access avenue. Like a mysterious volume that has fallen from the motorway, half-buried in the ground, the inclined box, which houses the multi-use hall beseeches the imagination of the passersby. The inclination of the roof is determined by the heights demanded by the different functions of the interior spaces.

The mast, the screen and the box, they are inscribed on the landscape according to the parameters of structuralism philosophy—point, line and plane."

Behind the façade's metal screen, there is a second skin of glass, and behind this, a wall, folded like a curtain. Each one of these successive skins describes a scenic plane. Sunlight during the day and artificial light at night reveal fleeting, imaginary spaces, improbable silhouettes and changing illusions of the building, similar to those undefined landscapes invented by a theatrical performance.

The dark and spectacularly-inclined box interpret the heights of the different areas—greater in the seating rows and less in the room for banquets and parties. Inserted between these two spaces is a stage of 9 by 12 metres and 8 metres high. This distribution allows the stage to use the banqueting hall as an auxiliary space or on the contrary, large parties can make use of the stage.

Nearly all the decisions made by Christian Drevet to shape the hall's interior (dimensions, distribution, materials, etc) were directed toward the achievement of good acoustics. The fact that the seating is fixed (although it is a multi-use hall) and the distance between the first row and the last, is only 13 meters, means that the sound-reception area is sufficiently small to permit it to be controlled with greater efficiency. In the same way, the walls are asymmetrical and the ceiling is covered with acoustic tiles.

At night, from a distance of one or two hundred meters, through the empty square, the metal screen, the glass façade and the apertures in the folded wall, a car driver or a late passer-by can see how a mute, detached party is taking place in the interior of this strange artefact.

15   16   17

18   19

12, 13, 14. Details of the sloping glass corner.

15. Inside the vestibule and foyer, with the bar in
the foreground.

16. The building has several superimposed skins.

17. Detail of the stairway.

18. View of the stage.

19. General view of the orchestra.

DRTE Arles

Jacques Filippi

Building: Routes, Transport and Equipment Management.

Location: Quartier Fourchon 13200 Arles, France.

Date: 1995.

Promoter: Depertament des Bouches du Rhône.

Cost: 12,000,000. francs.

Architect: Jacques Filippi.

Collaborators: Gay Puig (section supervisor),

Marciano (structure),

Garcia (plumbing and climatisation),

A.S. Ingenerie (electrical installation),

Test (landscape gardening).

The DRTE is a centre for the management, control and improvement of region infrastructures and equipment. In 1993, the Bouches du Rhône Department organised a restricted public competition for ideas for the construction of the building and it turned out that the winner was the youngest architect among those who presented ideas, Jacques Filippi. At 27 years of age, the DRTE was his first commission.

The building can be found in the outskirts of the city of Arles, between the highway and nature, in a commercial area of spread-out, disorderly buildings. Although the beginnings of a marvellous land can be sensed through the windows of the offices, there are also signs of an incoherent growth (precisely the situation that this building was designed to combat). The DRTE does not belong to the city, nor to the countryside, but to their frontier, to the outskirts, where the images take on greater severity and they become urgent and immediate.

The outlying area is organised from a car—in fact, one of the first drawings made by Jacques Filippi for the ideas competition, was a night vision of the building as from a car window. The architecture has to compete with the huge billboards, with the traffic signs and with the façades of the industrial warehouses. Thus, there is really no space for subtlety, but rather irony instead.

Even though some are strongly rooted in the south of France, Filippi has introduced references into the project which are completely remote to the architecture—the iconoclastic and anti-modern films of Jacques Tati (Jour de fête, Mon Oncle, Play time etc), the creations of the famous Arles fashion designer Christian Lacroix, the bullfights which are held in the city's Arena and the aesthetics of the fifties (rock music, chrome convertibles, the identification with youth and rebelliousness) which, when re-examined in the nineties, completely change their meaning, there is no longer anxiety nor transgression, but only humour.

1. Plan of location.

2. Section.

3. West elevation.

4. East elevation.

5. Upper floor.

6. Lower floor.

7. South elevation.

8. North elevation.

9. View from the entrapped water.

10. The guard's house.

11. Nighttime view.

12. Filippi's project recalls certain aspects of the Ville Savoye revisited with a touch of irony.

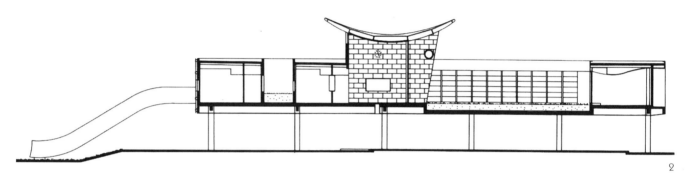

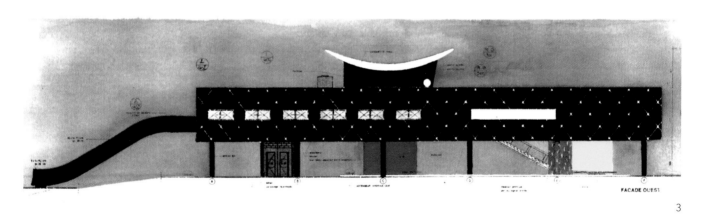

FACADE OUEST

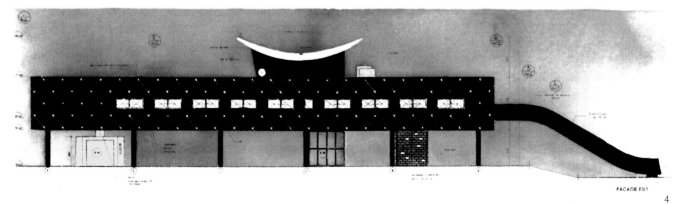

FACADE EST

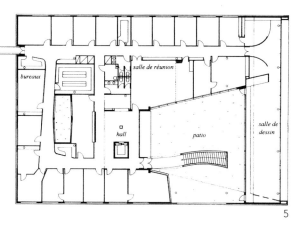

bureaux

salle de réunion

hall

patio

salle de dessin

5

41

9

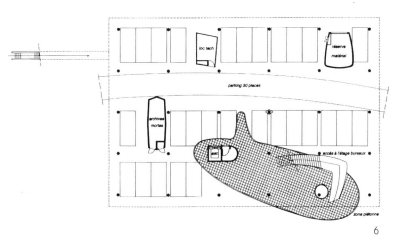

loc. tech.

réserve matériel

parking 30 places

archives mortes

accès à l'étage bureaux

zone piétonne

6

10

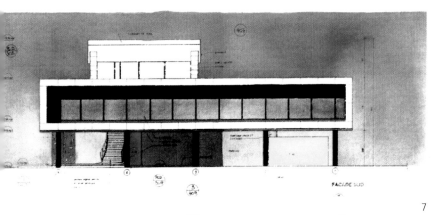

FACADE SUD

7

11

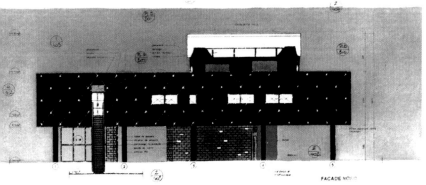

FACADE NORD

8

12

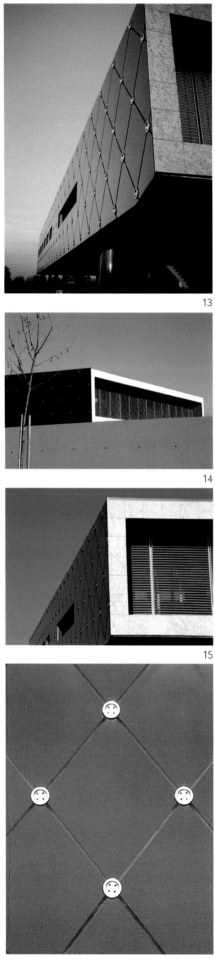

13

14

15

16

Filippi understands that in some countries it is not possible to act from architecture and that it is neccessary to look for other sources, since the impressions do not have anything to do with geometry or with the topography, nor with the town planning layout. The perception is not even direct—reality is a reference, a door, which gives access to cinematographic images. In another of Jacques Filippi's drawings, the building appears as a black mass which emerges from between the ares of wild wheat and white horns, like the half moon at night. The building takes on the appearence of a bull—the covering of aluminium sheets has been lacquered in black, the stairs leading to the first floor look like the tail and the skylight which illuminates the central part of the building resembles its horns.

Moreover, across this black skin is superimposed a silver network of buttoned-up rhomboid strips, just like the Provenzal clothing in the Barroque period and which are also found in many of Christian Lacroix's creations.

The building's interior is dominated by intense, lively colours, by stressed contrasts—surfaces painted in yellow, red or blue, and ceramic tile paving drawing a chessboard or mosaics of different colours. Filippi unveils the festive and playful side of modern architetcure—what is the subject of gags in Tati is used by Filippi to transmit happiness and humour to the spaces.

Nevertheless, there is also an architectonic strategy together with this sum of meanings. As in nearly all this region, the water table is found almost at the surface. In this actual case, it is only fifty centimetres from the surface, which meant that the plot was practically a swamp where water would flow with a simple kick on the ground. The foundations were made by driving piles to a depth of 15 metres below the ground.

The structure is therefore a reticulum of 7 x 6-metre round pillars. The ground floor is more or less open. The floor level has been raised by a metre to avoid flooding and this space under the office block is used as a car park. The rows of cars are broken up by pieces painted in brilliant primary colours which house the lifts, stores and other installations.

The reticulum of pillars holds up a 40 x 27 x 4 rectangular slab that holds all the offices. A 200 m² trapezoid-shaped patio has been cut out of the constructed surface and planted with a lawn. The access stairs from the car park to this floor lead to this interior garden. The individual offices can be found along the whole perimeter, except the south façade, where the draughting room (27 x 5 metres) crosses the building from one end to the other. The interior corridor which provides access to the offices is dotted with a series of linked elements that transmit vitality—a cloakroom, shelves, a small, north-orientated patio to provide illumination, a slight rotation in one of the stretches of walls, the curvature of the false ceiling etc.

13. DRTE Arles is Jacques Filippi's first project.

14, 15, 16. The black aluminum facade and stainless steel buttons evoke the costumes of the troubadours of the south of France.

17. Drawing room.

18. Patio on the upper floor.

19. Foyer on the upper floor.

20. Entrance stairway.

21. Elevator.

17

18

19

20

21

Centraal Beheer

Herman Hertzberger

Location: Apeldoorn, The Netherlands.

Completion date: 1995.

Client: Centraal Beheer.

Collaborators: Dolf Floors, Dickens van der Werff, Jan van den Berg, Ariënne Matser.

Photographs: Lock Images.

The Centraal Beheer office building was constructed in 1972 by Herman Hertzberger. Over the years this original structure was modified and enlarged until, in 1990, it was decided that a more far-reaching intervention was necessary. The resulting project combined the construction of new office space with the integration of all the earlier operations.

Hertzberger's solution created a link between his original building (CB1) and the adjacent premises (CB2) designed by the architects Kaman and Davidse, which had been acquired by the company. The combined property had several entrances but lacked a defined reception area affording easy access to the different departments, where staff could attend to the ever-increasing flow of visitors. As a result, the company decided to create a new zone with a single entrance that would not only meet these functional needs, but would also be an emblematic entrance to the whole complex, reflecting the company's new image.

Hertzberger's new entrance is a monumental concrete portico bearing the company's name and aligned with the street. The concrete walls that support the huge inscribed beam have been rotated to follow the direction of the existing buildings, and in this manner point the way to the entrance of the outdoor garage. The beam supports a triangular canopy made of over-sized metal sections,

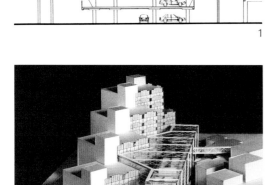

1

46

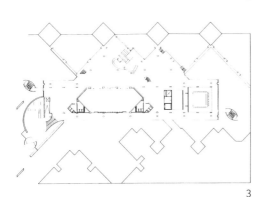

3

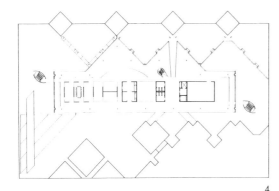

4

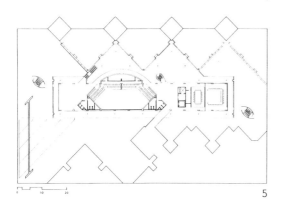

5

which leads the visitor from the entrance up to the large rectangular glass volume that houses the lobby.

The transparent new building, composed of a framework of pillars and metal girders supporting a glass roof and curtain wall, occupies the space between the two existing buildings. It breaks away from building CB1 at a 45 degree angle, extending outwards until it connects with building CB2 with which it forms a sawtooth shape. Inside this volume, we find another construction independent of the macrostructure, which constitutes the core of the new complex. This space is the new nerve center of the administrative complex and houses all the new services: a reception area, several meeting rooms, and a small congress center.

The result is an enclosed space, yet it is hard to say whether it is in reality interior or exterior. The triple-height lobby is framed by the free-standing volume that houses the services and by the façade of building CB2. Metal staircases, balconies that look out onto the atrium, walkways that span the void, halls and rooms all form a heterogeneous succession of spaces within a common order defined by the grid of the glass curtain wall and roof. Rather than resting directly on the ground, the new construction has been erected on top of a two-floor parking lot that already existed in the

6. Detail of the glass wall.

7. The steel structure is used as a jalousie to filter the light.

8. The railings are made of perforated metal sheet.

6

7

original project. The parking lot was left open to the outside in order to avoid the traditional dark, gloomy atmosphere of underground garages.

The program of the new area is distributed on three floors. The reception and the spaces used to welcome visitors are on the first level together with a modestly-sized, but superbly-equipped conference room. The public character and central location of this space led to an open design in which priority was given to the transit zones and wider spaces. Both this and the second floor are connected to the old building via two walkways, which determine the form of the double-height volume housing the conference room. The second floor is occupied by several rooms suitable for congresses and lobby areas, as well as the upper rows of seats in the conference room. On this floor, the shape of the rectangular, freestanding building and of CB2 can now be discerned. The third floor houses a series of meeting rooms and exterior lobbies common to the whole complex.

With the creation of this new central nucleus, people visiting the company's different departments enjoy improved communications through easy access to the new, public areas where the exterior reference to the two original buildings is not lost.

8

9

48

10

9. The corridors leading to the different halls in the extension act as balconies with views of the vestibule and, through the glass facade, of the street.

10, 11, 12, 13. One of the most eye-catching details are the staircases. All of them are different. They are designed as unique, almost sculptural objects. So the underlying philosophy is precisely the opposite to structuralism. They are not conceived as basic elements in a text (like in the original building). They are finished objects, with their own image. The overall image of the building is, however, coherent. The stairways, footbridges, perforated metal sheet surfaces, steel jalousies and glass all convey a uniform image. This gives rise to the opposite phenomenon to twenty-five years ago. At that time, the syntax of identical objects, articulated in different ways, was intended to promote diversity. In this new building, the sum of different elements produces a single image.

11

12

Palafolls Sports Pavilion

Arata Isozaki

LOCATION: PALAFOLLS, BARCELONA (SPAIN).

DATE OF COMPLETION: SEPTEMBER 1996.

CLIENT: PALAFOLLS TOWN COUNCIL.

ASSOCIATED ARCHITECTS: FRANCESC CORNELLÀ, LLIBERT ESTANYOL (SITE SUPERVISORS).

PROJECT TEAM: TOSHIAKI TANGE, MASATO HORI.

STRUCTURE: JULIO MARTÍNEZ CALZÓN, NILO LLETJOS.

PHOTOGRAPHS: EUGENI PONS

The commission for this small sports pavilion resulted from the success of Barcelona's Palau Sant Jordi, the main sports pavilion of the infrastructure built for the Olympic Games. Although on a much smaller scale, the theme was a similar one which meant that Isozaki was able to develop the same concept, though with very different solutions, for this new project.

The pavilion in Palafolls is situated on a site in a new area of town growth, with an almost rectangular perimeter and very few points of reference to its immediate surroundings. The pavilion is placed in a large circular outline measuring 81 square yards (67.5 meters) in diameter, with a blatant indifference to any possible references to its setting. This great circle, built with a low brick base, like the frame of a drum, will only be covered on the south side, giving the volume of the pavilion a hemispheric perimeter. The northern half thus becomes a spacious courtyard, establishing contact with the space inside the pavilion through a great window. This produces a complex of spaces consisting of the pavilion and a large outdoor area for community events.

The roof of the closed hemisphere follows the same concept as the Palau Sant Jordi: a ring around the perimeter gradually pushes up towards the center of the space, covered with a second, dome-shaped piece which conveys its load to the first ring. The basis for this concept, which is taken from traditional Byzantine forms of

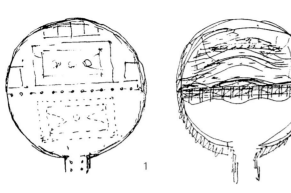

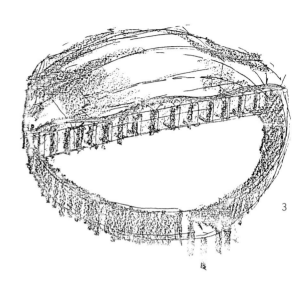

1

2

3

6

7

1, 2, 3, 4, 5. Preliminary sketches.

6. North elevation.

7. Side elevation.

8. Cross section.

9. Longitudinal section.

10. Site plan.

11. First floor.

12. Ground plan of tiered seating.

13, 14. Nighttime views of the translucent glass surface which closes in the north facade.

15. The sinuous profile of the roof is suggestive of many images: a wave, a cloud, a mountain…

16. Detail of the zinc sheet roof.

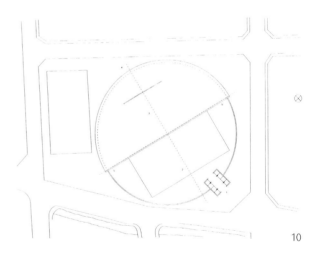

10

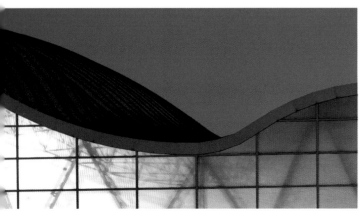

13

14

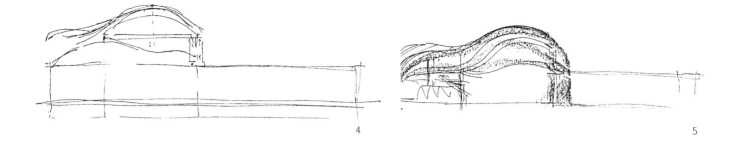

4

5

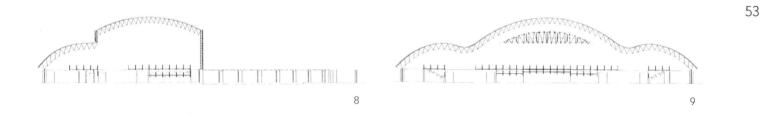

8

9

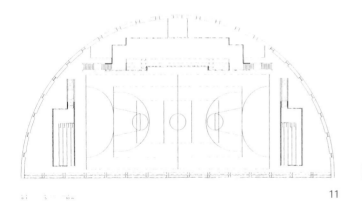

11

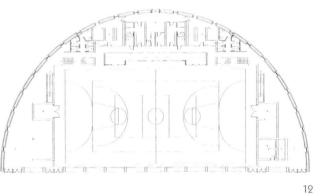

12

15

16

supporting domes, is the self-supporting behavior of any spherical form when closed in on itself. In this way, the first ring in the perimeter is able to bear the higher central dome as a result of its own self-supporting ability.

However, the use of these two rings is quite different from the one applied in Palau Sant Jordi, where the entire system is based on a series of stronger elements in the four corners which act as nerves. The smaller dimensions of this "little palace" in Palafolls mean that the whole roof surface can be covered using a completely isotropic mesh with no need for additional elements to reinforce it. This gives the covered space its own particular atmosphere, as the ethereal nature of the space frame appears to invade the whole expanse.

With the pavilion occupying the southern half of the circle, the window which segments the circle faces north, providing a suitable degree of indirect lighting. The outer surface of the roof is covered with sheet zinc, and the entire light shell rests on a triangular system of concrete pillars concealed by the brick wall which forms the drum base.

Isozaki remarks that the pavilion roof aspires to be a small hill which creates a visual link with the image of Palafolls castle in the background. In many of the project sketches, he represents the pavilion as a simple roof which projects down to the ground to complete the construction. Isozaki's interest in roofs as a determining element in any building finds a pretext for further investigation in this small pavilion.

It is interesting that Isozaki has on various occasions turned to the recourse of domes when they have been totally disregarded by the most orthodox currents in modern architecture. Only a few architects (such as Nervi or Candela) expressed an interest in these forms, using the technology of light, reinforced concrete plaques. Isozaki has on several occasions employed similar forms, using the techniques of the space frame or bar frame, which can be traced directly to Japanese tradition and its methods of design and construction of roofs.

54

17

18

19

17, 18, 19.

The sophisticated metal mesh of the roof is a continuation of Isozaki's research into this type of structure; the roof of the Sant Jordi stadium in Barcelona is another example.

20. Detail of the steel-tube mesh.

21. Entrance to the changing rooms.

Tobu Golf Club

Masayuki
Kurokawa

Location: Yubari-gun, Hokkaido, Japan.

Date of Construction: July, 1993.

Architects: Masayuki Kurokawa Architect & Associates.

Collaborators: Sasaki Structural Consultants and Nishida
Engineering Equipment, Kankyo Engineering Inc.
(structure), Matsushita Eletrical Works Ltd.

Photographs: Nacasa & Partners Inc.

"I wanted to design a building that looked like a hummock of soil, with the roof the same colour, like baked clay, gently resting on the rolling green golf course.

It should be unobtrusive, similar to a single-family house surrounded by the beautiful landscape of the Hokkaido region. In fact, the building ought to be a kind of big house, a house for golfers.

The club consists of a main building and an annex. The former is rectangular, with a rectangular open area in the middle. The annex's roof continues the slope of the main building so that they appear to be joined together. The club's relationship with its surroundings is all important: the building seems to lose itself in the natural environment. Its external appearance could be described as passive. In effect the building's design was dictated by the landscape.

However, once inside, the building's image completely changes. The central patio contains a large pond with water on a level with the ground. The area around the pond, the sitting room and a

corridor, are naturally lit by the patio. This open space is the very heart of the building; it works like a trap to capture the natural elements.

The wind dances over the water in the pond. When it is still the water's surface is like a mirror, creating virtual images thanks to the reflections. At times the wind causes whirlpools in the water and the images grow. The breeze makes the reflections on the walls and the corridor's ceiling come to life. In late afternoon, as twilight nears, this spectacle of magic images reaches its peak.

The annex, almost buried in the landscape, and the main building, surrounding the patio are the key elements. Yet there is a myriad of small spaces and isolated details which add nuances and are vital in giving the building personality.

The effect created by these spaces was painstakingly planned. Details such as the edge of the eaves on the roof, or the texture of the outside aluminum surfaces, were designed to reduce the building's impact on the landscape. The continuity between the water's surface in the pond and the swimming pool, separated by a glass wall helps to remove the usual barrier between inside and outside."

1. Detail of one of the pools which let light into the basement floor.

2,3. Day and nighttime view of the central court.

4, 5, 6. Masayuki Kurokawa leaves the indoor spaces of the club in half light.

7. View of the restaurant. One of the club's main services.

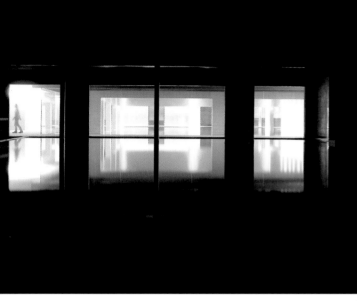

2

3

4

5

6

7

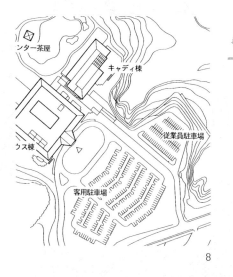

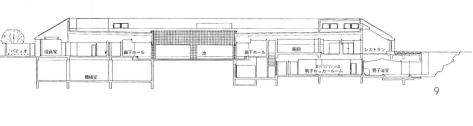

9

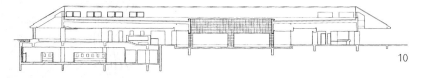

10

60

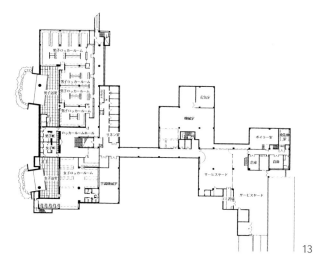

11

8. Plan showing location.

9, 10, 11. Sections. Kurokawa constructed a
low building so as not to interfere
with the landscape. Many of the
club's amenities are built below
ground.

12. First floor.

13. Second floor.

14. The concrete structure has been
left unclad.

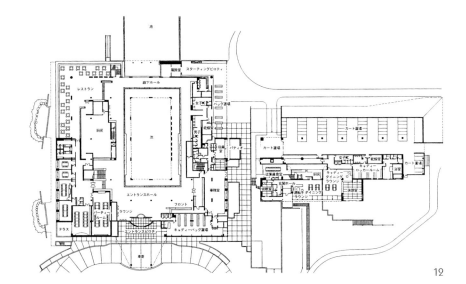

12

13

The Holz Altenried Exhibition Hall and Warehouse

Carlo Baumschlager, Dietmar Eberle

LOCATION: HERGATZ, ALEMANIA.

DATE OF CONSTRUCTION: 1995.

PROMOTER: ALTENRIED BERND.

ARCHITECTS: CARLO BAUMSCHLAGER, DIETMAR EBERLE.

COLLABORATORS: MICHAEL OHNEBERG (PROJECT),

OLIVER BALDAUF (SUPERVISION),

BÜRO PLANKEL (STRUCTURE).

PHOTOGRAPHS: EDUARD HUEBER.

The small German town of Hergatz is located in a very privileged position, close to the point on Lake Constance where the three borders of Germany, Switzerland and Austria meet. This is the spot where, traditionally, the members of three different countries, but with a common language, have come together. This is especially true of international relationships on a local level and these are the circumstances which encouraged the owner of the Holz Altenried timber company, with headquarters in Hergatz in Germany to study the local neighborhood of Voralberg in Austria as a possible site for the new industrial and commercial building.

The program consisted of the creation of a space dedicated to an exhibition hall and a warehouse together with a smaller area for offices and administration. Within the body of the building, the program was distributed as follows, the warehouse was confined to the lightless ground floor, whereas the lightsome upper floor contained the well-lit exhibition area and the core of offices, services and auxiliary rooms, all placed at the extreme western part of the building. The east face is a blind wall and it is the building's only flat façade to cater for any possible future enlargements of either the warehouse of the exhibition hall.

The other façades, as well as the roof, are somewhat convex on the exterior, as if the building's internal volume had swollen. The covering skin of wooden strips has been moulded in such a way so as to form a series of laminated wooden ribs which form the box shape of the curved walls. These ribs are prefabricated porticoes of spruce wood, each one having a distinct profile and the larchwood surfacing is constant throughout. There is no difference between the façade surfacing and that of the roof and with the exception of

the warehouse interior walls and the framework of the intermediate office floor, the material used, practically exclusively, is wood.

A large horizontal window has been incorporated into the façade which looks out onto the highway. Above it is the name of the company speled out in thin metal letters—an invitation to come and visit the warehouse and the exhibition hall. There is a concrete ramp that runs parallel to the building and leads to the entrance, which in fact, forms an integral part of the continuous large window. The opposite window, on the other hand, is more closed, having only a few round openings similar to the skylights in the roof.

The office and service sections of the building have narrow horizontal windows which are open in the corner and that provide this part of the volume with a distinct aspect—it becomes its head, the highest part, the part where the volume begins to decrease towards the east end.

Its organic shape, at the same time abstract, endows this project with the impression of an ark stranded in a post-industrial landscape. It reminds one of the lifeboat of biblical fame that has been transported to a new world. It is also capable of conjuring up some of the aerodynamic shapes of the fifties, which, in truth, had more to do with aesthetic movements than with real speed. This building is a primitive vessel sailing out of long-past times and, at the same time, the expression, shape and symbol of an irrefutable poetic modernism, both elegant and optimistic.

The elegance and dynamics of its form contradict the simplicity which dominates the interior space. Throughout its geometry and construction, the project continually suggests the work of craftsmen, as though it were a handmade object. This is undeniably in evidence where the exterior convex planes meet together to form the corners. It is also the case of the encounter between wall and roof, where the manual construction processes are both precise and exact.

There remains no doubt as to the reason for constructing this building—to announce the Holz-Altenried company and its association with wood. The simple strips of unworked larchwood, very typical of this timber region, are rather more than just a decorative facing. There is no question of a simple superficial rhetorical effect, but the expression of an economy and the workings of a company in an area of traditional development within the art of woodworking.

64

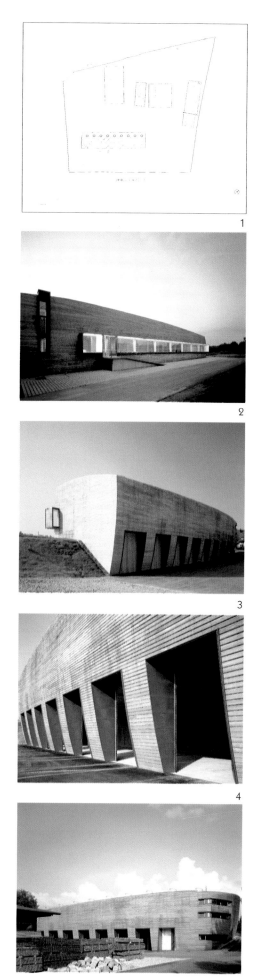

1

2

3

4

5

6

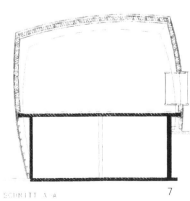

SCHNITT A A

7

1. Site plan.

2. View by night of the main facade.

3. Rear facade.

4. Close-up of the storehouse doors.

5. General view of the wood piles.

6. Detail of the entrance ramp and
   vertical window.

7. Cross section.

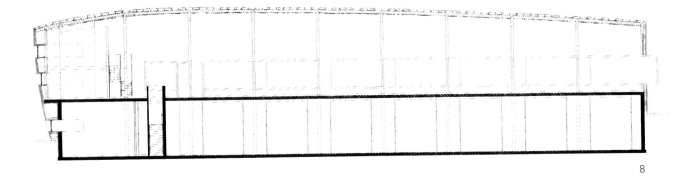

8

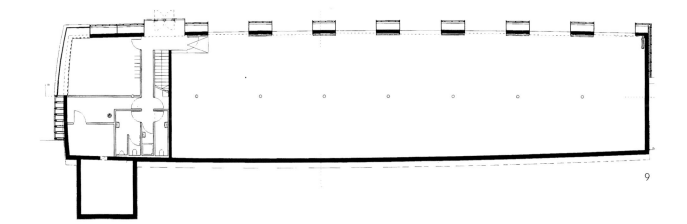

9

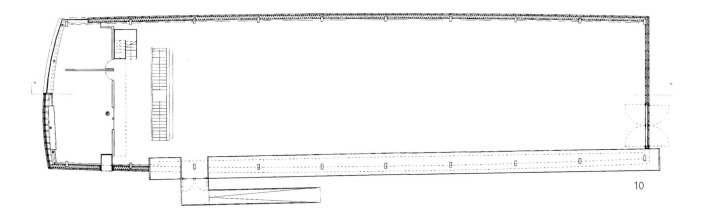

10

8. Longitudinal section.

9. First floor.

10. Second floor.

11. Inside the exhibition hall.

12. Interior detail of the vertical window.

13. General overview of the stairway and office modules.

11

12

13

Kol Ami Temple

William P. Bruder

Location: Scottsdale, Arizona, U.S.A.

Date of Construction: 1994.

Promoter: Temple Kol Ami.

Architect: William P. Bruder.

Collaborators: Wendell Burnette, Eric Robinson, Beau
Dromiack, Maryann Bloomfield,
Tim Wert (design team).

Photographs: Bill Timmerman.

The use of metaphors is a strategy that William P. Bruder, as he himself explains, learned from the architect Antoine Predock. Since then, he has converted its use into one of the constants within his work. Two recent examples are the Phoenix Central Library, whose copper covering brings to mind the local mining tradition, and the Riddell Design and Publicity Agency in Wyoming, whose form is similar to that of the straw lofts of the neighbouring farms. His projects are thus, in a certain way, translocations of lyrical situations or invocations.

The Kol Ami Temple displays spartan spaces which acquire their definitive value as from the very entrance of the light. William Bruder summons up all the meanings of natural light— its physical reality, its spiritual significance and its emotional capacity. In parallel, Bruder brings out as a counterpoint that which is precisely the opposite to light—material (texture, earth and place) poetic simplicity and plainness under the scorching desert sun.

The project puts forward the undertaking of a center for worship and learning in the form of an ancient village, in the spirit of the old communities of Masada and Jerusalem. A school and a Hebraic temple forming a fortified village which, two thousand years later, follows the same tradition of those desert communities, on another continent, in another desert.

2

3

1. The various buildings comprising this religious, educational and recreational center are laid out along streets and small plazas, like a village.

2. General view. The building blends in perfectly with the desert landscape of Arizona.

3, 4, 5. The temple is built out of the humblest materials: concrete block and corrugated polycarbonate sheet. Nonetheless, Bruder produces a finish which elevates these materials.

6, 7, 8. Following page: The building offers a fantastic response to Arizona's warm climate. The small windows and corrugated polycarbonate protect it from the sun's intense rays.

71

Those historical communities conjure up architectural images related to the generalised use of natural stone as an element for wall construction which has become an integral part of the desert landscape and has provided it with definite form. Taking into consideration the limitations imposed by such an extraordinarily low budget and the desire to include a strong symbolic presence, the emphasis for this center was placed on the use of concrete blocks as the essential construction element. It has been used as the finishing material, both inside and outside, it has not been surfaced and the expressive possibilities of its texture have been examined in depth. A particular image has been achieved through these methods—dry, irregular surfaces, worn down by high-pressure sand-blasting. They summon up pictures of age-old stone walls and produce a feeling of oneness with the earth.

The east wall, which gives onto the parking area garden, has a slight, sensual curve when seen from above, and in section it is inclined a few degrees towards the interior. So, the wall courses of this room progressively fall away, each one is placed slightly further inwards with respect to the previous one.

It is a simple, yet radical, operation. On the one hand, it provides the volume with an unquestionably sculptural character, and

4

5

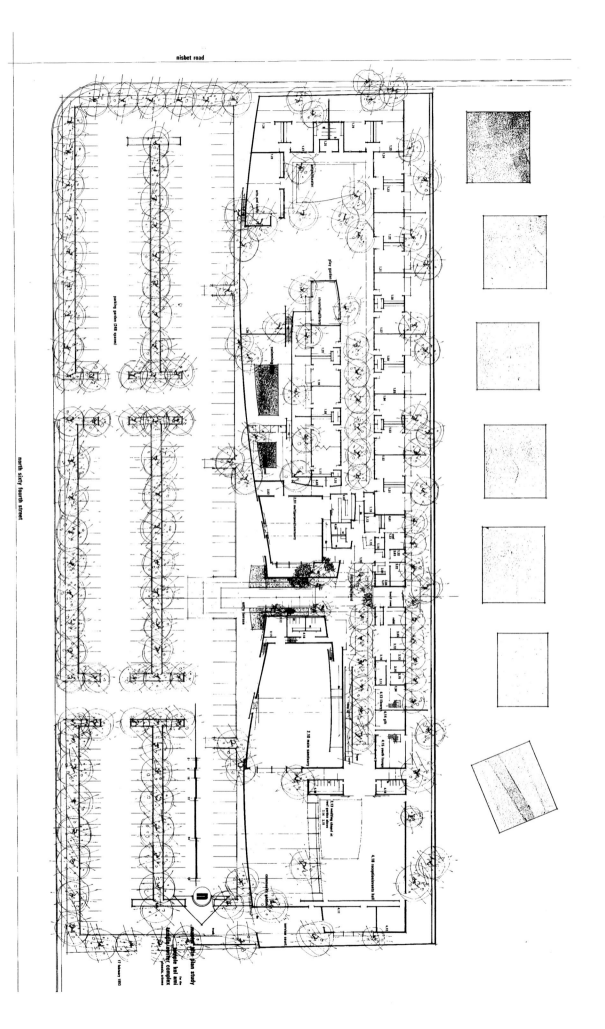

on the other, it enriches the interior space, achieving greater expressive capacity. This force is highlighted by the way in which natural light has been directed inside through openings in the roof.

There are exterior canopies to give protection from the light, which at the same time draw zigzag shapes on the walls. They are constructed from metal tubes and translucent uralite and under them a concrete path encircles the building.

The roof over the halls continues the profile of the exterior canopies and a line of light separates the sanctuary at its center and asserts at the same time the unity of the community and the holy identity of the place.

9. General floor plan.

10. View of one of the entrances.

11, 12. Two interior views of the main hall of the temple.

13. Most of the spaces have overhead lighting.

14. Detail of one of the halls.

75

10

11

12   13   14

Faculty of Journalism

Ignacio Vicens
José Antonio Ramos

LOCATION: PAMPLONA, SPAIN.

DESIGN DATE: 1994.

COMPLETION DATE: 1996.

ARCHITECT: IGNACIO VICENS, JOSÉ ANTONIO RAMOS.

COLLABORATORS: FERNANDO GIL, ADAM BLESNICK.

PHOTOGRAPHY: EUGENI PONS

The relationship between mass and void is what gives this building its form. From the point of view of the skin that is, the image, the volumes that stand out against the sky and the hollows that carry light into the concrete mass are equally important.

Studying the decisions that gave rise to this form reveals a twofold strategy. First, the various functional areas were to be split off into separate volumes. Therefore, as the functions of certain elements such as the ground floor main auditorium or the block containing the audio-video library became increasingly independent, they would tend to emerge as autonomous pieces. The second was that the architects were to endow each space with a specific kind of lighting and its own way of relating to the exterior. The exterior was to consist of openings and patios, as if the building had been constructed in negative from the roof downwards.

Consistent with the first strategy, Vicens and Ramos chose a homogeneous finish for the whole building (in concrete, a simple yet noble material) and they designed the windows as incisions or holes so as to lose their identity as windows. These decisions not only avoid contaminating the building's appearance with trivial details but also they are absolutely necessary if the observer is to fully appreciate the guiding principle of restraint.

The Social Sciences Faculty is located in an important part of the University of Navarra campus, next to the Library and the Law and Economics faculties. This is the center of gravity of university life, and for this very reason the architects were required to include a central plaza in their design. While the building was designed mainly to house the Faculty of Journalism, some of its lecture rooms were to be made available to students from other disciplines.

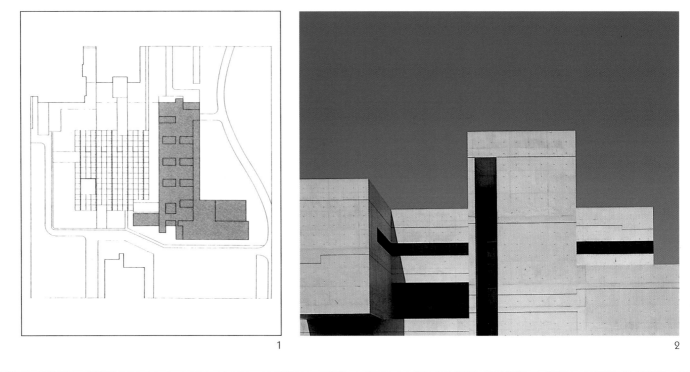

78

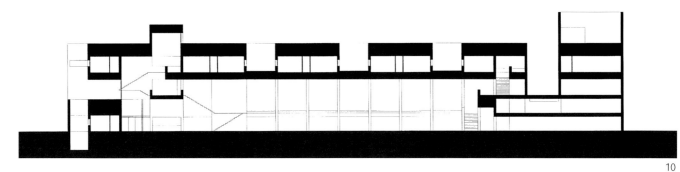

10

1. Plan of location.

2, 3, 4, 5. Detail of the openings.

6. Preliminary sketch.

7. Rear facade.

8

9

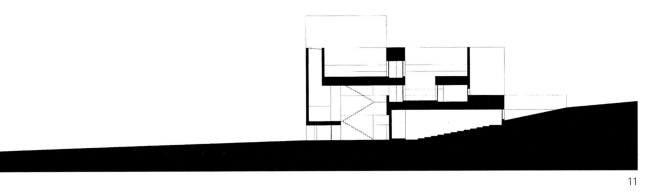

11

8. Facade over the plaza.

9. West-facing facade.

10. Longitudinal section.

11. Cross section.

12

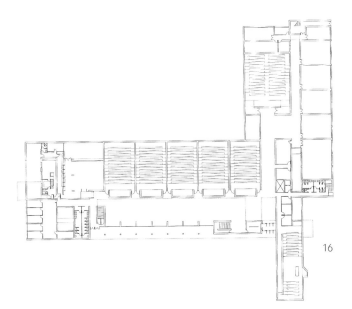

16

13

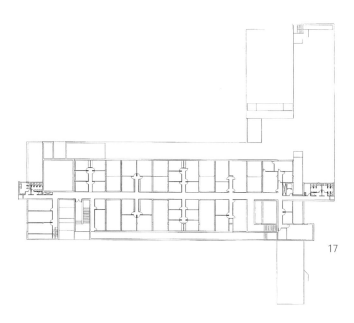

17

14

15

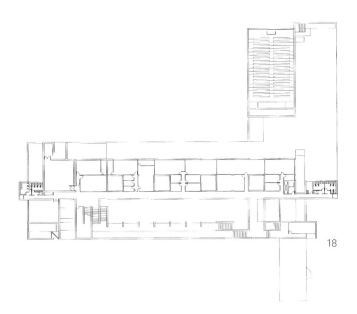

18

The functional program includes theoretical and practical workshops, radio and television studios, seminar rooms, an audio-video library, offices and a cafeteria. A clear division was needed between the corridors linking the spaces belonging exclusively to the journalism department and those shared by the other schools, which were all located on the ground floor.

The building layout lends to the overall design what in the opinion of the architects constitute the three fundamental activities of any university: research, transmission of knowledge, and living together.

Research, conducted by small groups in quiet rooms isolated from the rest of the institution, is an activity that the architects have designated for the fourth floor, structured according to a system of interior patios, paved with pebbles and empty except for an Acer japonica palmatum tree whose leaves change color.

For the second fundamental activity, the transmission of knowledge, lecture rooms are concentrated on the ground and second floors, oriented toward the north, with classroom facilities designed to accommodate theoretical and practical instruction.

Finally, the architects took into consideration a third activity that is often overlooked: living together with others. Chance encounters, informal conversations and relationships established outside of class hours are sometimes as important as the classes themselves. While professors and university authorities can do little to foster this activity, the architect can do much, since it is his or her responsibility to create the spaces in which it can take place.

For Ignacio Vicens and José Antonio Ramos, the faculty's main space is the multi-storied atrium leading to the lecture rooms. By virtue of its dimensions, its lighting, its links with the plaza, its visual relationships and the traffic patterns it establishes, this space constitutes the building' s main social center.

19

20

21

12. The main atrium.

13. All the walls are of bare concrete.

14. Auditorium.

15. Oblique view of the roof.

16. First floor.

17. Second floor.

18. Third floor.

19, 20 , 21. Details of lighting in the main atrium.

Faculty of Economics

Mecanoo

Location: Utrecht, The Netherlands

Date of Plan: 1991-1992

Construction Date: September, 1993 to May, 1995.

Client: Foundation Financing Exploitation Accommodation Uithof, Utrecht.

Builder: Hollandse Beton Maatschappij bv. Utrecht

Associated Artists: Gera van der Leun, Henk Metselaar, Linda Verkaaik.

Size of Construction: 23,500 square meters

The new building for the Faculty of Economics of Utrecht Polytechnical is located in a part of the Uithof campus which has come to be known as the "kasbah." Like the cities of Magreb, the area's urban characteristics are compactness, low building height and a marked introspection based on the use of interior patios. The more than 23,500 square meters of the new center are built around three patios and occupy only three floors.

From the beginning, the idea was to create a building that not only met the requirements of the educational program, but also gave students the opportunity to enjoy the building more fully. The provision of a large number of undefined spaces where students can talk, eat, and drink shows an understanding that these activities form just as much a part of student life as does studying.

Access is from the north side, where the areas of communal services such as meeting rooms, the multimedia library and the restaurant/café are wrapped by a smooth skin of glass. From here, a comb-like system of wings opens out, housing the Faculty's departments and administration on their perimeter, while the classrooms are grouped around the main patio in the central wings.

The north wing is undoubtedly one of the highlights of the design. The four closed boxes which house the various rooms are grouped under a glass roof. The four volumes can be seen through the roof, mixed with reflections of the city and the nearby canal. Each is finished with a different material and the interstices between them are clearly marked by the forthright nature of their design. The large sheet of glass forming the façade has its own metallic structure, which is independent of that supporting the four interior volumes, thus accentuating even more the difference between the enveloping skin and

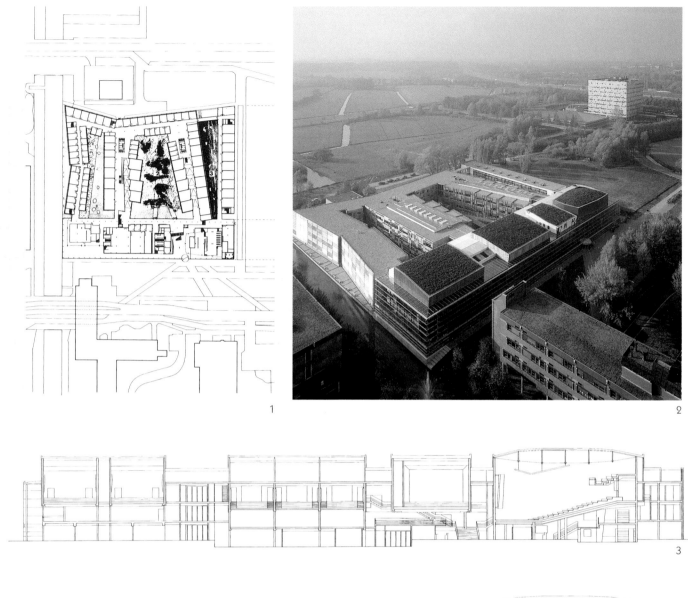

1

2

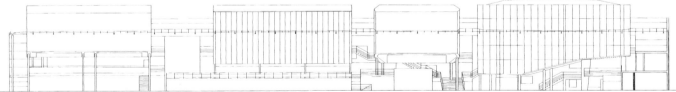

3

4

1. General ground plan.

2. Aerial view.

3. Section of the classrooms.

4. Section of the great
   glass foyer.

5. Nighttime view of the
   glass facade.

6. View of the facade over the canal.

7, 8. Sections of the ramp-corridors.

9. Jungle court. The footbridges cross
   between the bamboo plants.

what is contained within. The spaces which appear between the façade, the floor of varying height and the volumes of the enclosed rooms, form a series of corners and niches which can house a variety of activities.

The central hall gives access on all three floors to the corridors which lead to the classrooms, the various departments and the administration areas. The two central wings unfold in a succession of impressive ramps, some hanging from roof ties, which cross the narrow corridors and give access to the classrooms. The ramps are complemented by stairs lit by overhead lighting, which unite the different levels.

The markedly different characters of the patios in the center of the building imbue it with a variety of environments. The Zen patio, which takes its inspiration from notions of Japanese gardens, is covered by large rocks and two different types of gravel, while two delicate trees complete the calm oriental nature of the space. At the other end of the complex, the water patio has views of the surrounding canals and green fields. The reflections, the changing light, and the passing of the

5

6

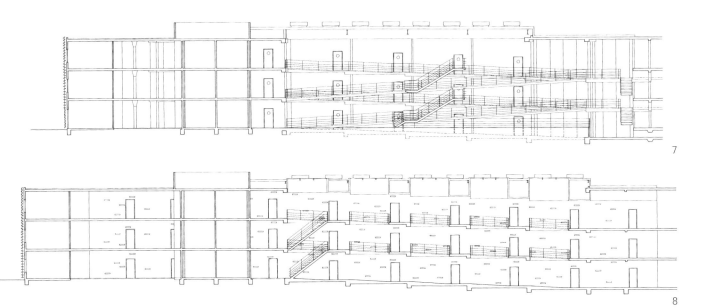

7

8

seasons ensure that its appearance is constantly in flux. The larger central patio has the most activity and movement. Its theme is the forest, and it is covered by bamboo of different varieties, heights, and colors. Crossed by walkways which connect the recreation areas grouped around it, the patio is a dynamic space, erasing the boundaries between the interior and exterior of the building.

The façades of the patios are also of different materials. Cedarwood lattices and panels of okumen surround the Zen patio. Glass and metalwork enclose the central one, while the water patio is faced with the same type of aluminum sheeting used for the perimeter of the building.

9

10

11

12

13

10. View of the main entrance.

11. Detail of the steel, aluminum and glass
     structure of the main facade.

12. Inside one of the corridors. A continuous
     table allows students to work with a view
     of one of the courts.

14

13. Detail of the concrete floor.

14. The scale of the building is reflected
     in the details.

15. First floor.

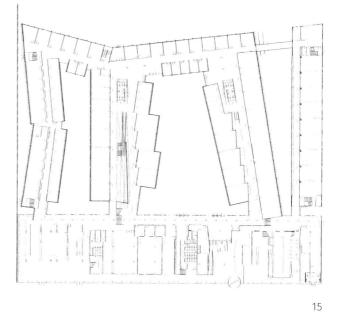

15

16. View of the Zen court.

17. Second floor.

18. Third floor.

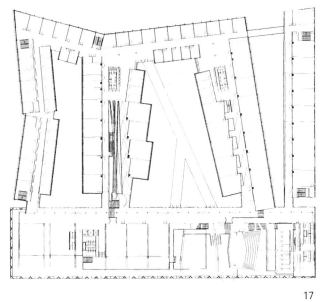

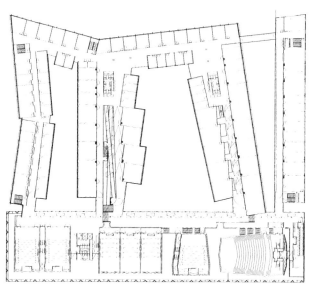

17

18

19

18. View of one of the corridors. The ramps are
slung from the ceiling with steel ties.

19. The classrooms are designed as huge volumes
which float over the atrium.

The Box

Eric Owen Moss

Location: Culver City, California. USA.

Date of construction: 1994.

Promoter: Frederick Norton Smith.

Architect: Eric Owen Moss.

Collaborators: Lucas Ríos, Scott Nakao, Scott Hunter, Eric Stultz, Todd Conversano, Sheng-yuan Hwang, Paul Groh, Thomas Ahn (Design team), Joe Kurily (structure), John Snyder (electricity), Peter Brown-Samitaur (constructor).

Photographs: Tom Bonner.

"What the devil are all those metal bars doing hanging in the air? This is the question you will ask yourself when you see the staircase from below. The answer escapes you. Then you cross a wall to reach the upper part of the roof just under the box and the wall hides the space you have just left. The bars no longer exist. But you can recall them in your mind, perhaps now that you can no longer see them, you will discover their meaning." - Eric Owen Moss.

In spite of their grandeur, the buildings of Eric Owen Moss are difficult to understand if you do not visit them and despite their excessive aspect, they are constructed with little material and with uniform finishes. The strength comes from their plasticity, from the flowing forms and from its implicit movement. They are full of play, of puzzles and spatial riddles.

The Box is not a building on a new site, but an appendage to an old industrial building which adapts itself to the typology of these spaces. The rest of the original warehouse has been re-covered and painted while waiting for a later intervention. Meanwhile, in the box, the space resists being closed in. The ground plan is rectangular and the structure is of wooden trusses with a central pillar and a longitudinal lintel.

The Box is definitely an element of very reduced dimensions, the size of a single-family house, if the area of the existing building is not taken into account. It has minimum functionality—the reception is on the ground floor and there is a meeting and conference room on the upper floor.

In concept it is a box (hence the name), but a box where things are beginning to happen (and this is Moss's game)—a slight inclination, the intersection with a cylinder on the ground floor, a formal track which leaves the actual path going up.

Spatially, it consists of three parts. First, there is the reception area, almost perfectly cylindrical, which cuts through the existing roof. Behind

1

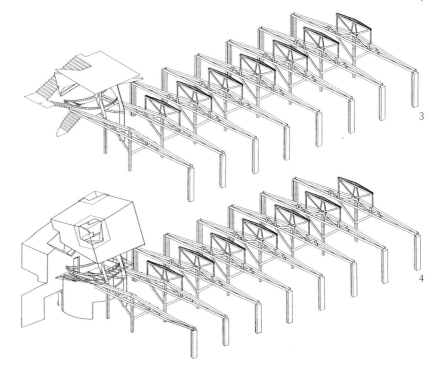

2

3

4

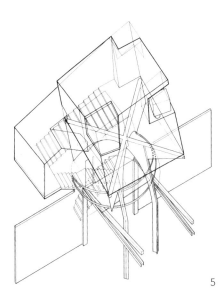

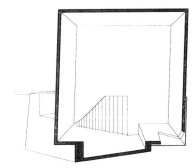

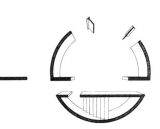

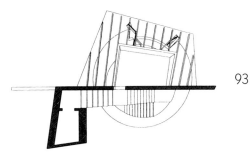

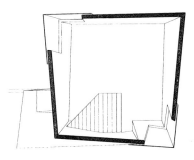

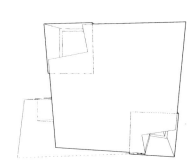

5

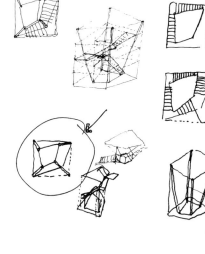

6

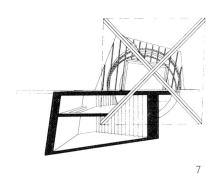

7

93

8

9

1. Nighttime view. Underlighting the building emphasizes its dramatism.

2, 3, 4, 5. Axonometric studies showing the geometric and constructive development of the building.

6. Preliminary sketches.

7. Floor plans.

8. Moss on the storehouse roof.

9. The corner window looks out over Culver City, while its opposite faces Beverly Hills.

10

11

12

the reception, an exterior staircase leads to a second level—a landing-balcony over the cylinder and under the central part of the box. The sectioned part of the roof is glass-covered, thus illuminating the reception area. From this level an interior staircase rises to the third level, a space which has been set aside as a conference room.

The intersection between the upper volume and the inferior cylinder favours the appearance of a series of very complicated constructive elements. For instance, the reception area cylinder cuts the wooden truss structure of the existing industrial building. However, the segments of the cut trusses are later replaced to show the selfsame intersection of the new building and the old. On the other hand, the two beams forming the crosspiece that supports the Box takes its shape from the successive macles between the volumes which were planned by Eric Owen Moss on the initial sketches. The lower part describes a circumference which is the result of sectioning a sphere, the base of which would be the cylinder through the two planes of the crosspieces. Thanks to this operation, the beams are converted into arches that rest on the ground.

In the words of Moss, the windows are analogies of the same box. They are placed at two opposite corners of the conference room. By occupying the corners they are not plane elements, but volumetric ones. Moreover, there is no carpentry, so that they are perceived as solid glass.

The finishes of all the surfaces are uniform and monochromatic—smoothed grey cement stucco. There are no differences between the inside and the outside, between the walls and the ceilings, as if it were a piece that had come out of a sculptor's mould.

The west window looks toward Culver City. In the opposite corner, the window orientated to the east offers views of the palm trees on the crest of Beverly Hills.

10. The building is practically monochrome. The various
        finishes are all different shades of gray.

11, 12. The architecture of Eric Owen Moss emerges from
        the technical development of his preliminary sketches.

13. Detail of the first floor.

14. Moss' architecture is a difficult one to furnish.
        It would be like placing a chair on top of
        a sculpture.

13

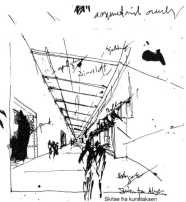
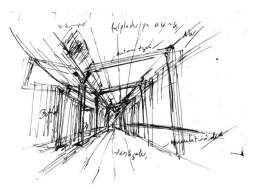

Skitse fra kunstaksen

Arken Museum of Modern Art

Søren Robert Lund

LOCATION: ARKEN, DINAMARCA.

CONSTRUCTION DATE: 1996.

ARCHITECT: SØREN ROBERT LUND.

COLLABORATORS: ELGI THORODDSON, JORGEN ERICHSEN, METTE ADERSEN, FINN BOGSTED.

PHOTOGRAPHS: FRIEDRICH BUSAM/ARCHITEKTURPHOTO.

An architectural design that excels in creating links between art and architecture is that of museums of modern art. They are spaces in which architecture interacts with art, thus giving rising to interesting, and at times ambiguous, relationships. Art enriches the formal repertory of architecture and enhances its communicative capacity. Creative proposals are tempered by the rigor of the project, while promoting freedom of expression.

The Arken Museum of Modern Art summarizes the two tendencies that evolved in Scandinavia during the 1960s, 1970s, and 1980s. One of these tendencies is expressed in Robert Lund' s project, which takes up the influence of the "new empiricism" of Alvar Aalto. This architectural movement was a reaction against the excessive planning of architecture during the 1930s. It is an attempt at spontaneity, adapting buildings to traditional materials and their location. It places the habits and needs of human beings at the center of interest. It is an attempt to recover domestic comfort and an everyday feeling for texture and color. Lund, like Aalto, imbues each part of the building with an identity, creating a layout in which each function is assigned to a different element, though all are inseparably interwoven.

The second tendency evolving in Scandinavia, as it appears in the Arken Museum of Modern Art, is also a result of the so-called "new formal abstraction," which favors architecture that is both figurative

1

2

3

4

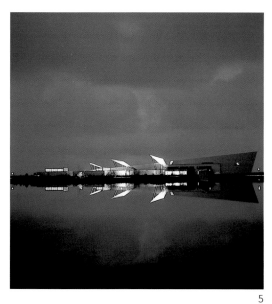

5

6

1. Lund starts out from the metaphor of a shipwreck.

2,3. Sections.

4. Søren Robert Lund won the ideas competition when he was just 26 years old.

5. Nighttime view.

6. View of the entrance.

7. Detail of the marquees.

8,9. Two views of the restaurant volume.

7

8

9

10. The main hall.

11. General ground plan.

12. The spaces are dramatic
    in character.

10

11

13. The footbridge offers a different view of the paintings.

14. Detail of one of the skylights in the rectangular halls.

15. The elevator which compensates for the small difference in level between the two galleries could be an installation.

16. The architecture purposely influences our perception of the works on display.

and abstract at the same time. It is based on the interplay of forms and dynamic representation of space. The interplay of forms constitutes both the starting point and the final result. This leads to an architecture of different fragments, volumes, dynamic constructions. At the same time, it signifies a break with history and tradition, and an attempt to forget established symbols and connotations.

In this type of architecture, the first sketches which reflect the creative act are of special importance, as is the final result. Robert Lund uses the metaphor of a shipwreck as the starting point for the creative process, integrating it into the history of the landscape. The museum stretches out over the sand dunes, a large, horizontal volume, forming an axis that organizes the volumes of the exhibition rooms. The entrance becomes progressively smaller as the visitor advances from the wide, open landscape into a familiar, "intimate" atmosphere, like the entrance to a church.

Visitors may choose between two routes, located on the same level: the art axis leads them through a sequence of exhibition galleries with skylights and openings that look out onto the landscape. Or, via the Foyer, a second route leads through space designed for complementary activities: theater rooms, projection rooms, and the restaurant.

The scale of the project is in proportion to the surrounding elements. Each space is accorded a proportion depending on its purpose, light, and acoustics. Lund was sensitive to the ruggedness of the surrounding area and chose uncovered concrete to create the building's texture. This rough skin contrasts with the façades and metal skylights to enrich the overall effect. Here, Lund reveals his great capacity for renovating forms of architectural representation. The classical system of plan, section, and elevation is consistently rejected in favor of other possibilities, such as using lines as a metaphorical language to lead us to a space brimming with images.

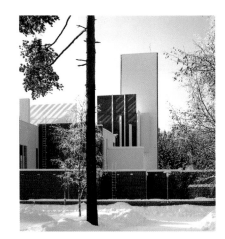

Männistön Church
and Parish Center

Juha Leiviskä

Location: Kuopio, Finland.

Completion date: 1993.

Promoter: Lutheran parish – Kuopio evangelist.

Architect: Juha Leiviskä.

Collaborators: Pekka Kivisalo (planning),
Parkku Pääkkönen y Mirja Arias
(artist), Harry Dunkel
(structural engineer), Markkanen & Tiirikainen
(mechanical engineer), E. Pitkänen & K
(electrical engineer).

Photographs: Arno de la Chapelle, Jussi Tiainen.

A work like Männistön Church goes beyond architecture. Its construction could never have involved cement trucks, workers, cranes and scaffolding. Although someone may have seen people working on it, it is more probable that this was only an illusion born of habit and inattention, because it does not seem possible that this building was constructed by man.

It is almost certain that the church is a crystallization of the music from the organ it now houses. It looks as if the air that was buffeted and pushed through the organ pipes, after hanging motionless in space to produce the music, and ending up as a sediment of white material that has gradually formed the walls.

This explanation is, of course, only a hypothesis. It is possible to doubt its truth when observing the building from the outside (because one might think that the church forms a natural part of the landscape), but once the visitor enters the building it becomes absolutely clear that it could only have been produced by the music.

It is clear therefore, that this church differs from most churches; not only is it dedicated to God, but God played an active role in its construction. Juha Leiviskä does not work like other architects; he has an advantage, he works in a state of Grace. "I put a lot of effort into ensuring that all the elements that make up the space –the walls (and the artworks decorating them), the roof, the first floor amphitheater and the organ– combine to form a single entity. My intention was to

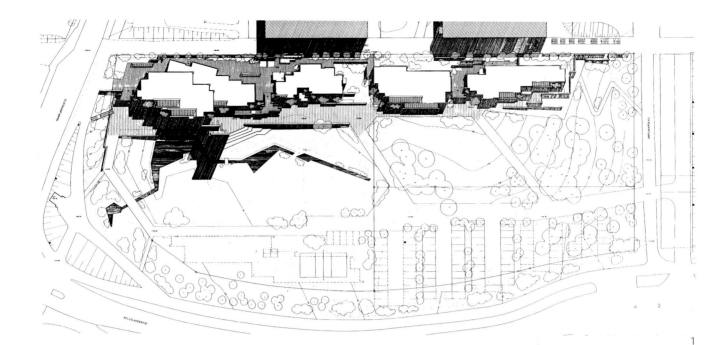

1. Plan of location.

2,3,4,5. Cross sections.

6. Facade overlooking the street.

7. Facade overlooking the park.

8. Detail of the entrance.

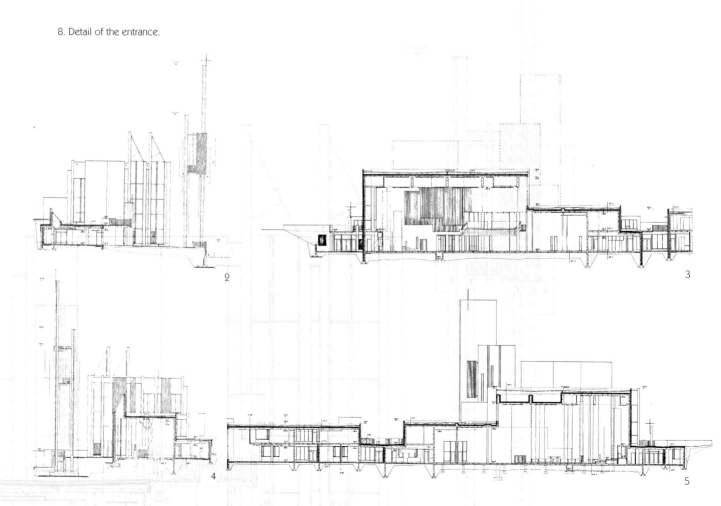

6

7

8

favor the essential interaction between large and small, open and closed, high and low, and to use the spaces as instruments to interpret light – the veil woven by reflections and their continuous variation."

Leiviskä's proximity to the Baroque world (with Lutheran asceticism and never with the suffering and punishment of the Counter Reformation) is not so much aesthetic as epistemological. He identifies artistic experience with religion and mysticism. This is why it is admissible to say that his work goes beyond architecture, because the final object is not the space itself, but rather to show revelation as a reality.

From the point of view of town planning, Leiviskä's aim was to achieve a stable spatial environment combining the existing surroundings and the new buildings though layered growth; fragments of a city on a human scale.

The sloping site of the church, the parish center and the social center is located on a strip bordered by several high apartment blocks built in 1960 on one side, and a park on the other. Due to the incline, there is a 3.5 meter difference in the elevation of the two sides of the elongated site.

The main door, which leads out onto a terrace overlooking the park, is on the lower level. Light penetrates through its many folds. A foyer functions as a transitional space between the entrance and the main body of the church, which is an inner space with an imprecise outline. This foyer, a narrow and quite dark space adjacent to the retaining wall on the west side, connects the entrance to the rear of the building where there is an entrance into the church proper (this made it possible to orient the altar to the east). This space provides a moment of silence and reorientation between the outside world and the church. It is decorated with water colors by Mirja Airas depicting scenes from the life of Paavo Ruotsalainen (the founder of the Finnish Pietistic Movement).

The composition of the interior spaces is structured around the natural light. Leiviskä explains, "I sought an artistic economy based on the progressive growth of the effect of the light. The main body of the church, and in particular the altar, represent the climax of this progression".

The eastern orientation of the altar takes advantage of the more intense light during the morning service. Markku Pääkkönen's design for the altar was based on the reflected light and uses subtle strips of color. The materialization of such an ethereal element as light is the main architectural strategy used to create a spiritual atmosphere.

107

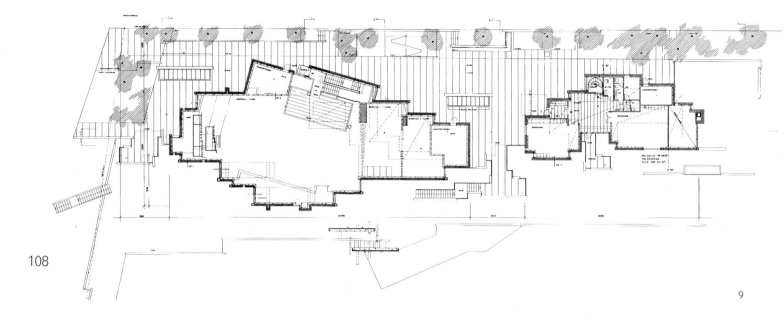

9

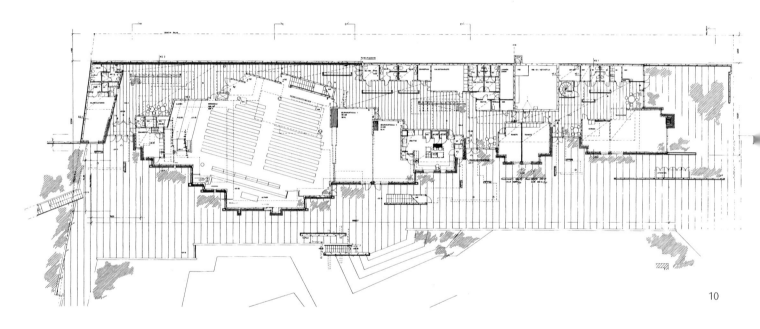

10

11   12   13   14

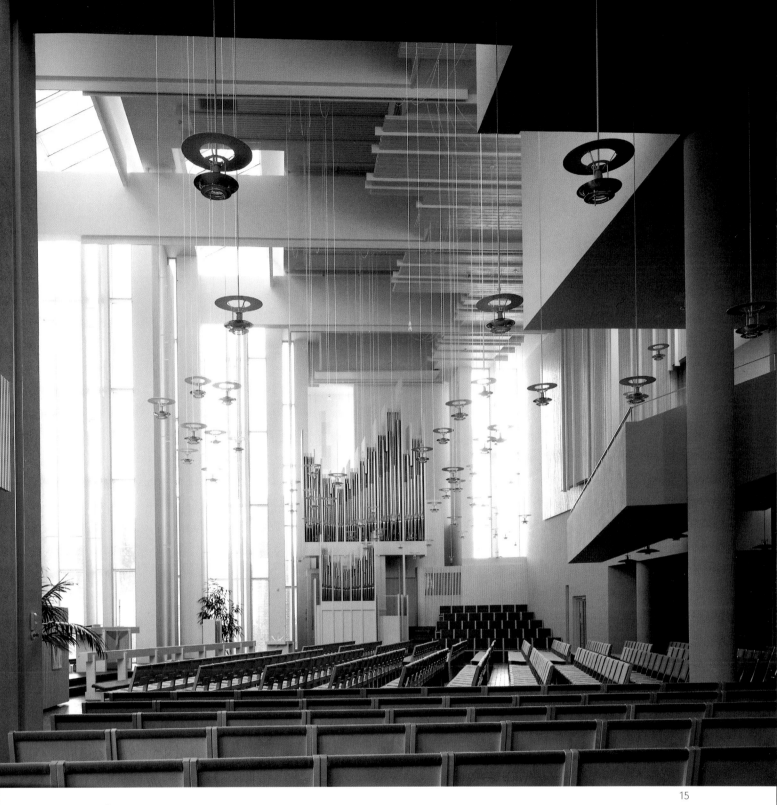

9. Upper floor.

10. First floor.

11,12,13. The hall folds like a sound
wave.

14,15. Leiviskä builds the space
around indefinite regions
of light and shadow.

Kaze-no-Oka Crematorium

Fumihiko Maki & Associates

LOCATION: NAKATSU, JAPAN.

DATE OF CONSTRUCTION: 1995-1997.

ARCHITECT: FUMIHIKO MAKI & ASSOCIATES.

CLIENT: NAKATSU CITY COUNCIL.

COLLABORATORS: SASAKI ENVIRONMENT DESIGN OFFICE (LANDSCAPE).

PHOTOGRAPHS: NÁCASA & PARTNERS INC.

From the beginning, the construction of a new crematorium in an area of beautiful countryside on the outskirts of the Japanese city of Nakatsu was conceived as a collaborative project between a firm of architects and one of landscape architecture. This collaboration was designed to ensure that instead of both firms working separately and later uniting their work, the project would be a joint venture from the very beginning. In this way, the design possibilities would be multiplied, as the architecture of the building would become a landscape element, integrated in an overall design which consisted of the careful construction of a new landscape.

The crematorium building itself consists of a one-story edifice characterized by its horizontality, whose profile, which is visible from the park, becomes one of the principal elements of the new landscape. The profile consists of three main parts: the inclined volume of the chapel (the highest point of the complex); a blind, sloping crowning wall which encloses some of the functional areas of the crematorium; and a porch which both separates and unites the other two elements. Behind this screen, the design of the crematorium proper occupies a generous space and is scrupulously organized according to the functional requirements of funeral rites. However, even the organization of the interior forms a precise kind of landscape: by strict control of the light allowed in, of the pattern of patios, of the ponds, the openings and the screens, a walk through the interior acquires all the qualities of a landscape experience. In this way, the interior too becomes a part of the park, which is not simply limited to the planted areas but embraces the entire site. In contrast, the green areas of the park receive a treatment with clearly architectural connotations, with a distinct center being created in the form of an elliptic area which sinks into the ground as one approaches.

1. The strategy of placing objects behind sloping surfaces is repeated. This places visitors very firmly in a given spot, creating depths and avoiding a global reading of the entire area at all costs.

2, 3. The building's outline seen from the park is one of the elements which shape the overall landscape.

4, 5. The footpaths complete the building's outline.

6. Plan of location.

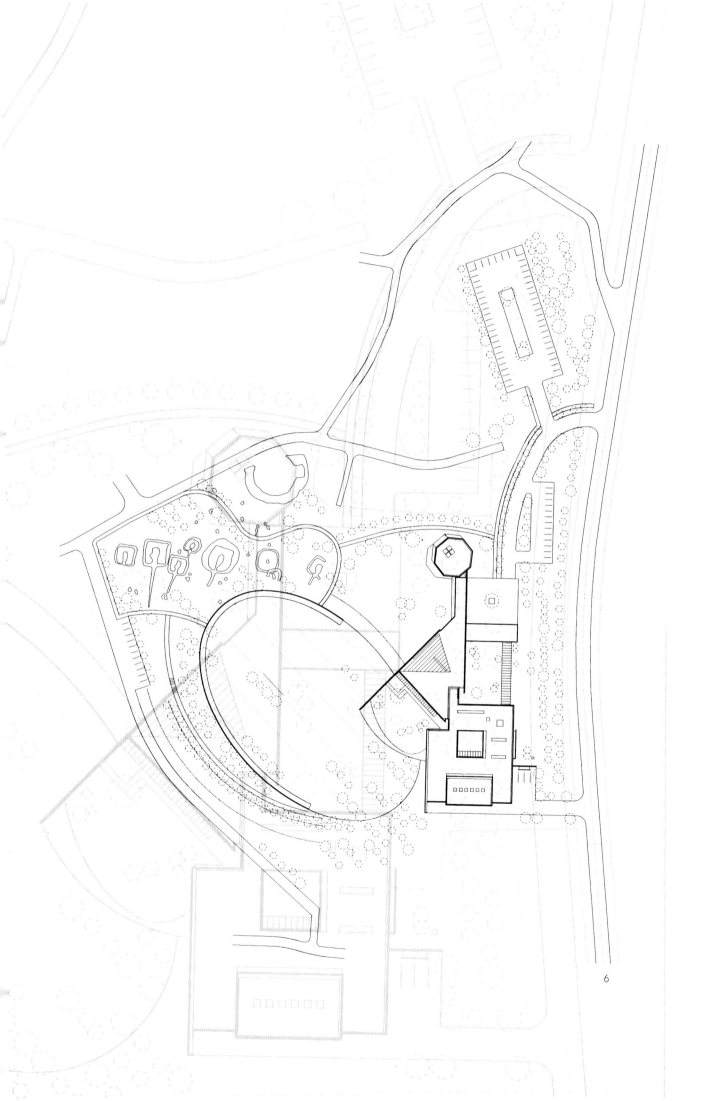

7

7. The inside of the crematorium is conceived as a landscape made up of connected places. Discrimination of the various components (the presence of the sky, water or the walls) defines this landscape by the application of the architecture's resources.

8. Although there are no direct references, the spiritual importance of the landscape recalls Asplund crematorium.

9, 10, 11. The spartan simplicity of the interiors encourages asceticism.

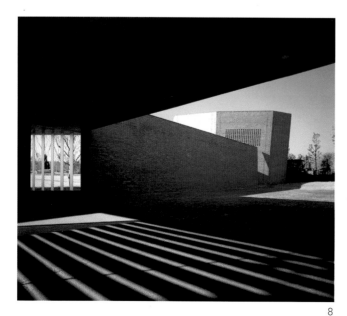

8

9

10

11

The form of the ellipse overlaps the layout of the crematorium building, suggesting an interwoven geometric system, the third part of which is composed of a series of ancient sepulchers that were discovered before the project commenced, and which, although occupying a separate area, also interweave with the ellipse and thus with the overall design.

Architectural methods and landscape instruments are mixed and combined throughout the site meaning that the architecture becomes a mechanism for the construction of a landscape, while the landscape constantly resorts to architectural mechanisms. The design of the park makes clever use of changes in the paving, isolated elements such as the trees, extremely rigid geometric topographical patterns, etc. The idea of vertical movement is ever-present: in the building this is conveyed by the openings, and in the park by the rises and falls in level which culminate in the low point in the middle of the ellipse, which seems to draw together all the elements. The inclined volume of the chapel appears to question this fundamental feeling of verticality in an apparent renunciation of the most intrinsic qualities of architecture.

While the various routes through the park are organized with a planimetric abstraction which is never sufficient to determine the nature of the project, the real point of view at which the design is aimed is the horizontal vision of the spectator. Even the crematorium building seems to have been designed as an elevation. There is a total emphasis on the views generated by the design, with objects such as the building, the trees and the walls repeatedly emerging from behind a grade, and other objects being hidden behind a smoothly inclining slope. The authentic plane of the design is the elevation and the numerous sections, which assume the traditional role of the ground plan. The same happens in the interior of the crematorium: the height of the openings, the spaces and the wall panels exploit all the possibilities offered by the vertical dimension.

117

12. General ground plan.

1. Parking lot.

2. Patio.

3. Entrance porch.

4. Oratory.

5. Crematorium.

6. Vigil room.

7. Patio.

8. Waiting room.

9. Offices.

10. Chapel.

11. Park.

12

Private homes

Residential architecture is much more conservative than its public counterpart. The same person who sets forward an audacious proposal for a modern building would question the suitability of using this formal line of research when it comes to building their own house. For a long time, most innovations in the field of residential architec-ture took place in second homes with their more relaxed lifestyles and less strict programs.

The houses we present in the following pages are all incontestably architectonic in quality and point up how a little extra effort in planning an a freer rein to creativity ultimately produce more interesting, stimulating spaces, where everyday life becomes less one-dimensional and anodyne.

Villa Wilbrink

Ben van Berkel

LOCATION: A. AALTOSTRAAT, AMEERSFOORT, NETHERLANDS.

COMPLETION DATE: 1994.

ARCHITECT: BEN VAN BERKEL.

COLLABORATORS: AAD KROM (PROJECT COORDINATOR),
PAUL VAN DER ERVE, BRANIMIR MEDIC (DESIGN TEAM),
BV AANNEMINGSMAATSCHAPPIJ ABM,
BUREAU BOUWPARTNERS (CONSULTANTS).

PHOTOGRAPHERS: HÉLÈNE BISNET, KIM ZWARTS.

In this small family house situated in a district of Amersfoort in the Netherlands, architect Ben van Berkel has turned a few traditional notions about suburban housing upside-down. No rose garden, no lawn to mow, no views across the street, no neighbors peering in. A salutary solution to life on the outskirts perhaps. Certainly one would not expect anything less from Ben van Berkel and Caroline Bos, the dynamic partnership from Amsterdam, responsible for some profound explorations of architectural theory in recent years and the realization of some high-profile projects, including the Erasmus Bridge in Rotterdam.

It was apparently the client's aversion to gardening that played an important part in the design. As the architects comment:"The house was stretched out, using up as much land as possible with a limited program, so as to avoid the presence of a garden." As a result the roof begins at the outer limit of the plot at street level and rises gently in an oblique plane. The only concession to a garden is a patch of shingle at the rear of the house, where some low-maintenance trees are planted in regimented fashion.

The oblique roof planes, covered in chunky, industrial gravel, present an austere appearance to the outsider, revealing little of the domestic life within. One feels the inhabitants are hunkering down inside this protective outer layer, like an animal within its shell. The different angles of the slope down to the garage and the upward slope of the roof reinforce this impression.

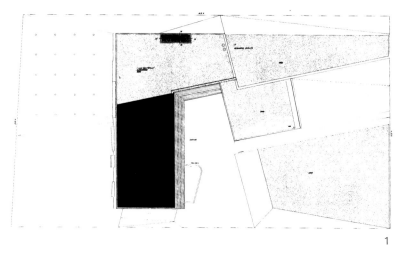

1. Plan of the roof.

2. Entrance between mortar brick walls.

3. Overview of the central court. The space is almost domestic in scale, functioning as an open-air room.

4. The wooden-clad volume of the bathroom emerges into the court.

122

Once inside though there is an unexpected luminosity and clarity. The entrance, concealed in the middle of the oblique planes, is approached by a narrow path running between the garage and one of the gravel-covered slopes which leads to an inner courtyard. This is the core of the house: the quite small dwelling space is arranged in an L-shape around it. The hall leads directly into dining/kitchen area and on to living room which gives on to the rear; the bedroom wing, with a raised floor level to distinguish it, runs along the rear of the house. Within the privacy of the courtyard the extensive use of glass allows the natural light into the interior. Apart from a large, slanting window in the north facade, the outward-looking windows in the living area function more as interesting graphic features than for illumination, carefully designed to preserve privacy: an oblique horizontal strip in the kitchen parallels the sloping roof; a floor-level window in the living room becomes a focal point. The bedroom windows protrude slightly, encased in wood, disrupting the impeccably smooth surface of the rear wall, while an eye-level slit in the exterior wood-clad bathroom wall makes it an intriguing presence in the patio.

The exterior walls are clad in sand-limestone bricks which are glued rather than pointed. The effect is of a tough, rugged structure which combined with the gravel gives a very textured appearence. The interior provides a soothing contrast, with its smooth surfaces, light colored wood and minimal decoration.

This inward-looking contemporary urban patio house shuns its external surroundings to focus better on the life within it. Unlike many contemporary suburban properties, which are put on a pedestal for public admiration, Villa Wilbrink seems to have a more genuine response.

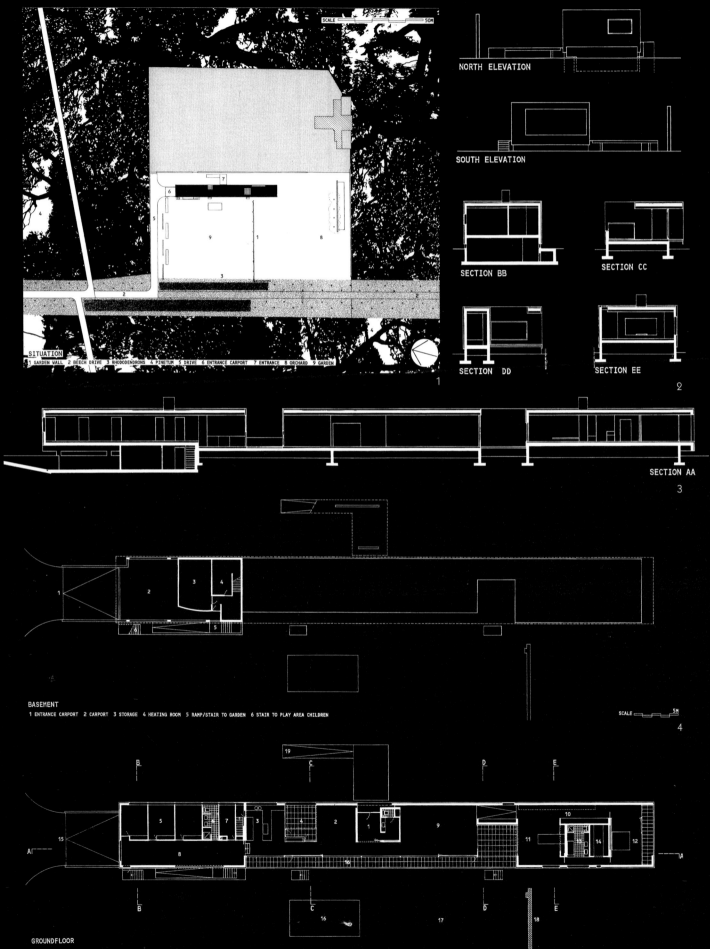

SCALE 50M

NORTH ELEVATION

SOUTH ELEVATION

SECTION BB

SECTION CC

SECTION DD

SECTION EE

SITUATION
1 GARDEN WALL 2 BEECH DRIVE 3 RHODODENDRONS 4 PINETUM 5 DRIVE 6 ENTRANCE CARPORT 7 ENTRANCE 8 ORCHARD 9 GARDEN

SECTION AA

BASEMENT
1 ENTRANCE CARPORT 2 CARPORT 3 STORAGE 4 HEATING ROOM 5 RAMP/STAIR TO GARDEN 6 STAIR TO PLAY AREA CHILDREN

SCALE 5M

GROUNDFLOOR
1 ENTRANCE 2 DINING 3 KITCHEN 4 PATIO 5 BEDROOM CHILD 6 BATHROOM 7 LAUNDRY 8 PLAY AREA 9 LIVING 10 LIBRARY 11 FIRE PLACE
12 BEDROOM PARENTS 13 BATHROOM 14 DRESSING 15 ENTRANCE CARPORT 16 TERRACE 17 GARDEN 18 WALL 19 RAMP TO ENTRANCE

SCALE 5M

1
2
3
4
5

6

7

8

9

back (brick wall) of the house. The rear façade is practically blind, except for a continuous window (which corresponds to the bedrooms) and the door. The garden façade, on the other hand, features large openings and terraces. The long façades are finished with red cedar, and the end walls with anodized aluminum sheeting.

The garage is the only element on a different level. It is in a semi basement, which is connected to the kitchen by a flight of stairs. In fact, the house is slightly elevated above ground level. The space between the ground and house is open, creating a line of shadow that makes it appear to be suspended in mid air.

As the light begins to fade, the inside of the house takes on the appearance of a stage setting when seen from the garden. Through the huge expanses of glass, one can follow the movements of the occupants from one room to another as if they were characters in a silent play being performed on a wooden dais. From inside, the immense windows frame the landscape like paintings only disturbed by the slight fluttering of the leaves in the wind.

Although the design of this house seems, at first glance, illogical because of the size and proportions, closer examination reveals countless possible relationships, both inside the house and between the interior and exterior. Rather than being the result of a merely functional organization, these relationships are generated through the introduction of irrational and instinctive values into the design.

To combine a desire for neutrality with a daring design, and to relate the house to its surroundings by way of an independent alliance; these two ideas were present from the outset, and were constant references that informed the whole design process.

129

1. Plan of location.

2. Cross sections.

3. Longitudinal section.

4. Basement floor.

5. First floor.

6. Facade overlooking the garden.

7. Rear and entrance facade.

8. The fact that the house is raised above the site means that there is no direct relationship, producing a sensation of distance.

9. View of the room with the fireplace, beside the master bedroom.

Huf House

Ernst Beneder

LOCATION: BLINDENMARKT, LOWER AUSTRIA, AUSTRIA.

CONSTRUCTION DATE: 1990-1993.

CLIENT/PROMOTOR: DR. JOSEF AND DRA. MARIA HUF.

ARCHITECT: ERNST BENEDER.

COLLABORATOR: ANJA FISCHER.

PHOTOGRAPHER: MARGHERIDA SPILUTINI.

Ernst Beneder was born in Waidhofen, Ybbs, and studied architecture at the TU in Vienna and the Tokyo Institute of Technology, where he met Kazuo Shinohara. Subsequently, he taught at both these institutions, and also at the University of Illinois. He is a member of the Japanese Society for the Promotion of Science and of various advisory boards, including the Austrian Society for Architecture. He has worked in architecture since 1988, some of his most outstanding projects being the rehabilitation of the town hall and an urban planning scheme in his home town, and the construction of a number of single-family dwellings.

Huf House (1990-1993) presents a simple layout covering a surface area of 800 square feet and was designed as a second home for a doctor couple in Blindenmarkt, in Lower Austria. The property, close to the dank woods lining the Ybbs River, is situated beside a large artificial pond and bordered by two roads which cross at an acute angle. It lies level with the roads, but slopes down to the pond, a determining characteristic of the site.

Geometry comes into play, establishing relationships with the site. The bisector of the angle becomes the gravel drive, once past the wall at the intersection of the roads, also the vertex of the property. This wall at the entrance, on the west, is the only boundary marker, and performs a purely symbolic function. It is freestanding and low, and serves mainly to frame the gate. Around the rest of the property there is no more boundary between asphalt and lawn than the trees. The body of the house can therefore be seen from both roads, particularly on the northern side, where the vegetation is sparser. The facade on that side is blind, and seems to rest squarely on the ground, which appears uniformly flat. However, a gap can be perceived between the ground and the prism — a hint that below this level there is more than meets the eye.

132

1. Spectacular projection of the house out over the lake.

2,3. Path leading to the entrance under the marquee.

4. The north facade is completely hermetic. The volume of the bathroom is clad in corrugated metal sheet.

5. View of the lake from the terrace.

6. Stairway leading to the terrace on the roof.

7,8. Two views of the rear patio.

9. The kitchen is right behind the entrance.

10. Plan of location.

1

2

3

4

5

6

7

8

The gravel drive goes on past grass and trees and ends in a flight of steps down to the pond. Before this, a sort of transverse canopy over the drive marks the entrance to the house. A large side entrance leads directly into the courtyard, also gravel, at the western end, and the dining room, floored with gray tiles, through a glass wall. The interior of the prism is conceived as a single space with objects arranged around it. The staircase, which connects the courtyard to the roof, sweeps past the fireplace and the deep-red kitchen unit with great naturalness. Viewed from the entrance, the staircase seems to be interior; it is in the courtyard that its appearance changes, taking on an outdoor look for the first time. As well as the side entrance, the prism presents two more openings at the front, in the form of windows.

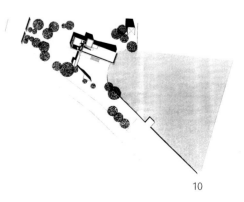

10

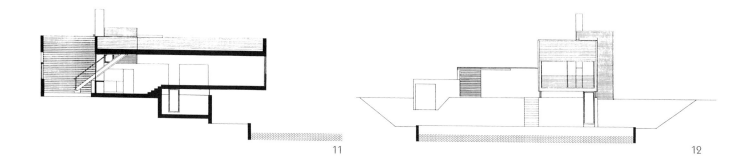

11   12

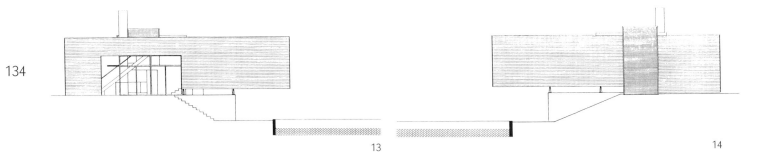

13   14

15

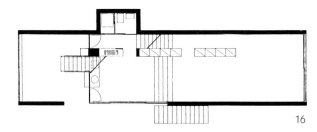

16

17

The privacy afforded by the translucent window in the courtyard, open to the sky, the stairs passing by the dining room, the continuity of the gray flooring, the glass and the strongly colored furnishings as subtle dividing elements, all result in the different parts — indoor and outdoor — blending into a single environment.

Yet the project is more, or perhaps less, than the purity of the prism. It has a sunken concrete base and a mottled aluminum tower containing the bathroom on the ground floor and a gallery-cum-bedroom on an intermediate level. The bathroom is outside the perimeter of the prism, separated by a frosted glass door. One of the bedroom windows is small and square and overlooks the courtyard; the other is narrower and looks out over the terrace and the dining room through the staircase.

On the north side, a narrow strip delimited by cupboards includes the staircases (one above the other) which provide access to the dark inner room and the bedroom. On the south, an extension of the entrance canopy covers the outdoor storage room, built-in wooden planking, with a wall that curves round to adapt to the irregular ground. The window on the eastern end, overlooking the pond, focuses the longitudinal perspective of the prism. In order to approach this window one must change planes. Just where the ground outside starts to drop, the floor inside gains height by five steps and its surface changes to parquet in the living room.

The horizontal strips of larch wood facing lend the facades a rough gray appearance rather like that of concrete. In the courtyard a timber frame gives warmth to this open space and acts as a louver blind over the window, casting an intimate, shadowy pattern. The same effect occurs at the window overlooking the pond, in this case due to metal railings.

The project seems to be in tune with the reflection of the bare branches in the water. The whole house breathes the same sense of tranquillity as the setting itself. At the same time it is a geometric abstraction that celebrates the changes in ground level and explains them. The internal circulation is a route which unravels.

The courtyard, the tower, the side entrance, the dining room; they all belong to the upper plane of the terrain, like the gravel. The living room, however, belongs only to the prism, the interior. The five wooden steps mark the change in plane.

11. Longitudinal section.

12. Elevation from the lake.

13. South elevation.

14. North elevation.

15. Gray tones dominate the interior.

16. First floor.

17. Floor plan of the roof.

18. The paving and some walls are in bare concrete.

135

18

House at Na Xemena

Ramon Estebe

LOCATION: IBIZA, SPAIN.

COMPLETION DATE: 1997.

ARCHITECT: RAMON ESTEVE.

COLLABORATORS: JUAN A. FERRERO, ANTONIO CALVO.

PHOTOGRAPHER: RAMON ESTEVE.

Na Xemena, located in the Northeast of the Mediterranean island of Ibiza, is a privileged location for any building. In this stark, rocky landscape by the sea, with cliffs that jut out into the Mediterranean, light is the dominant, enduring element. The grandeur and natural balance of this timeless panorama are awe-inspiring, and the unity of the building and its surroundings is no less so. This merging of a construction with its environment is the essence of the seductive and enduring power of great architecture.

The initial planning of the building, involving the choice of colors, materials, volumes and other elements of construction, was fluid and natural. No rigid geometrical scheme was imposed, although the design has a solid rational basis. The house is planned in such a way that it can be constantly expanded following the pattern of the original nucleus. The interior rooms have varying sizes and shapes and are added onto the main body following an upward path.

The construction climbs up the rocky base as a simple, compact whole running parallel to the shape of the cliff. From the outside, the arrangement of the terraces and the swimming pool leads the eye to the rotund shapes of the house. The whole complex strives to be a logical and unobtrusive extension of the landscape, in harmony with its surroundings. The different levels bring dynamism to the complex and delineate the outside areas such as the terraces and the swimming pool. These areas face the sea, which guarantees the unique light of the Mediterranean at all hours of the day.

The clean, basic exterior walls are perforated in order to capture the light, following a natural order determined by the interior arrangement of the rooms, with solid space predominating over the emptiness of the openings. The colors used for the exterior are obtained from natu-

ral pigments: gray for the floors and terraces and indigo for the vertical surfaces.

Three large windows made of iroco wood are embedded in the walls, framing the panorama of the terraces and swimming pool. The pool appears as a sheet of water which fuses with the sea. The interior walls, in white and cobalt blue, act as a unifying element throughout the house and are illuminated from above by the skylights.

A series of spaces leads from one to the other towards the exterior, with a sublime deference for their natural surroundings. This construction is a prime example of the importance of building with the environment instead of against it. Any setting is fragile and has a limited capacity for absorbing new images without being diluted by them. A receptive and carefully meditated consideration of the surroundings is essential in order to capture all of the implications of the topography, the sea, and the sunlight. The legitimacy that time has granted to this place can only be fully understood by prolonged contact with silence, with light and shadow, with day and night, and with land and sea.

1. The stairway during
   construction.

2. Preliminary sketch.

3. Volumetric model.

4. Ground plan.

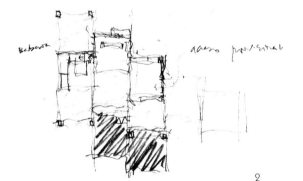

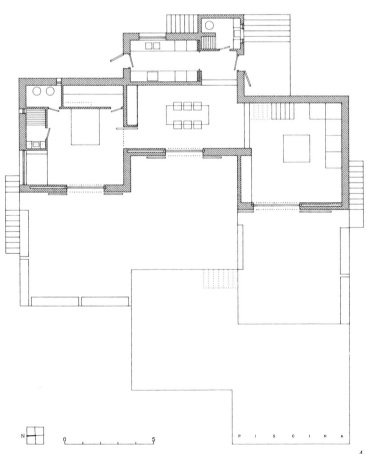

138

5

6

7

8

9

10

12

11

13

5. View of the terrace from the bedroom.

6. The furnishings are kept to a minimum.

7, 8. General view of the interior, organized over several levels.

9. The house is paved with polished cement.

10. Detail of the bath tub.

11. Almost all the wood used here is iroco.

12, 13. Stairway leading to the attic.

Stein Residence

Seth Stein

Location: Kensington, London.

Completion date: 1996.

Client: Seth Stein.

Architect: Seth Stein.

Photographs: Richard Davies.

Kensington is a residential district in London's West End characterized by rows of Victorian houses with gardens. Seth Stein and his wife acquired a stables built in 1880, which consisted of a group of rather industrial buildings laid out in U-shaped arrangement at one end of a site about 50 meters long. The rest of the space had previously been used as a paddock. The buildings had been used as stables until 1990, and when the Steins purchased the property they were in dreadful condition. The local authorities had been planning to completely demolish these buildings and construct new offices on the site.

Seth Stein, however, used the old stables and the nearly empty site for the construction of his own home. He had no intention of breaking away from the style of the existing buildings, nor from the traditional typology and appearance of the urban landscape. He preferred to work on the historical canvas, to set up a dialogue and a continuity with it. The first task was the painstaking re-construction of all the original buildings. The new structure was to exist side by side with them.

The daytime area of the house is situated at ground level. The shape of the building on this level gives rise to a long, interior courtyard and a transition space on the street side, suitable for parking. A walkway, made of dark, wooden panels runs along one of the walls of this space and leads to the front door. Around the ent-

1. The concrete cylinder, housing the bathroom, and the pink wall concealing a small junk room, are inserted just behind the entrance.

2. The side corridor leads straight into the living room without passing through the dining room, which is on the other side of the patio.

3. Central patio.

4. The wall is used as a backdrop for pictures, as though it were an art gallery.

5. Detail of the dining room, with the open-plan kitchen in the rear.

144

rance, paving slabs surround a white stone flower bed, and the white, transparent slats of a pergola shelter the door and throw striped shadows across the side walls.

Just inside the door, a rose-colored wall and a concrete cylinder narrow the space to form an empty reception area. The cylinder, which was poured *in situ* and polished, contains a bathroom, and is repeated on the roof. The rose color was specially scanned and prepared from a shade used by Matisse in his collages. In front of the rear wall of the courtyard, the space splits. On one side a glass-covered gallery along the courtyard leads directly to the living room at the end of the site. On the other side, the L-shaped, pink wall leads to a spacious area that houses the kitchen and dining room.

The interior courtyard is the central element in the design. It allows natural light into all the essential areas of the house, is a visual centerpiece, and ensures privacy by screening the house from the street. Seth Stein designed it not as a garden, but rather as an outside living space, a sheltered area where the children can play in the open air, a place to eat, or simply a scene to be looked at. This courtyard, which is five meters wide and very long, ends at a large staircase leading to the roof. The living room is an irregular space measuring about 9 m². Half of this room is covered by a glass roof set in a braced light steel structure, which spans the U-shaped space created by the brick façades of the old stables. In one corner a staircase following an existing curved wall leads up to the second floor. At the top of the stairs, a narrow corridor gives access to the bedrooms, whose walls support the wooden trusses of the original roof, an expression of the coexistence of old and new.

6. The living room has a large skylight.

7. Detail of the stairway leading to the third floor.

8. The stairway adapts to one of the house's existing corners.

9. First floor.

10. Upper floor.

11. Detail of the bathroom.

12. Master bedroom.

9

10

11

12

The Flower House

Peter Romaniuk

Location: London, United Kingdom.

Completion date: 1997.

Architects: Peter Romaniuk.

Collaborators: Tim McFarlane (structure),

Jeff Parkes (installations),

Ralph Pryke Partnership (constructor).

Photographer: Dennis Gilbert/VIEW.

Judging by the number of contemporary architects who cite the "Case Study" houses built in California in the fifties and sixties as the source of their inspiration, they must stand high in any ranking of :"Great Architectural Influences of Today."

In this case, London architect Peter Romaniuk was not faced with uneven desert terrain, or a sloping hillside; there were not even magnificent views that had to be maximised, but the concept was still appropriate. Romaniuk and his wife, Paula Pryke, had acquired a very tight urban site in a typical Victorian street in central London to build their own home; it also had to accommodate a workshop where Pryke, an internationally recognised florist, could work and run a flower school.

They were keen to have as much light as can be achieved in the midst of an urban setting without relinquishing privacy. Like generations of designers faced with a brief for an individual house, Peter Romaniuk claims he was greatly influenced by the "Case Study" houses built by architects such as Neutra and Koenig.

The house is a modern steel-framed building with a workshop on the ground floor and a two-story residence above. The proximity of neighbors is inevitable in such a central location in London, where terraced houses look onto each other across the street and through their rear windows, but not unavoidable as Romaniuk ingeniously shows. He designed the house so they could figuratively turn their back on the neighbors. It faces one way, to the East, in a radical move away from the traditional front and rear of most housing. Also as the residential part of the building begins on the first floor and is set back, the home is one stage removed from street bustle.

The substantial first-floor terrace, giving on to the street, reinforces the inner privacy but at the same time is an appealing outlet, a rare luxury for an inner-city property. The plan is fiercely simple and rational. The architect

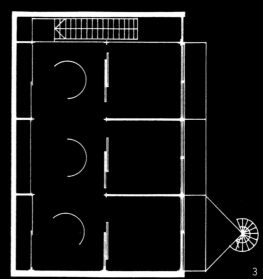

1

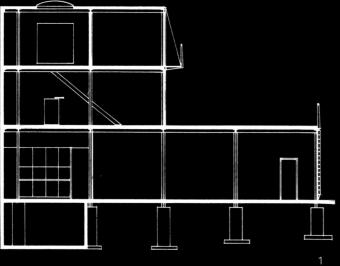

3

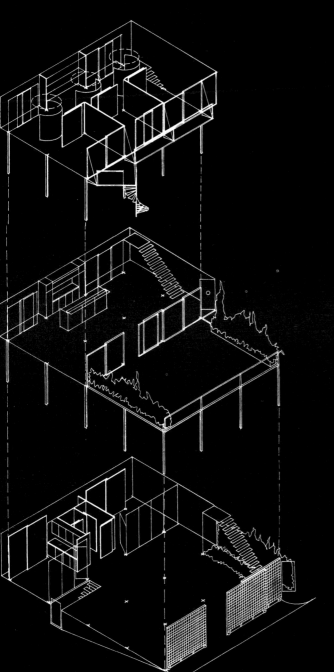

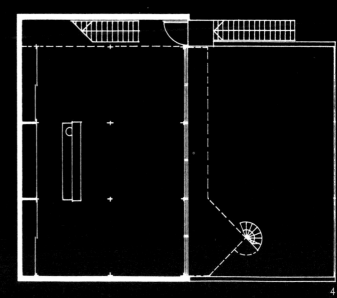

4

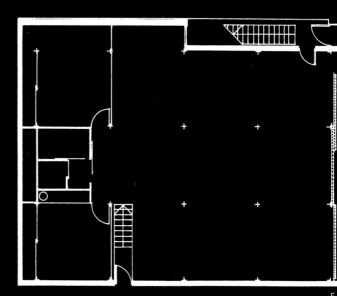

2

6

7

8

9

10

was determined the building structure should be clearly expressed. He created a modular system that suited both the work space and home, and the different elements – walls, ceiling, floor, steel frame, stairs – are all treated in the same way. The result is a homogeneous building with esthetic and structural echoes between workshop and residence, and between first and second floors.

The structural steel frame is set on a 3.6 x 3.6 meter grid. Mies-style cruciform columns are bolted to twin back-to-back steel angle beams. There is a certain pragmatic nature to this house, seen in various aspects but neatly illustrated by one detail of its construction: the beams were split to reduce their weight so two men could handle them, thereby avoiding the expense and inconvenience of a crane. The member sizes were carefully chosen for their good Hp/A factors to reduce the thickness of the instrument coating to a minimum. Two layers of profiled steel decking riveted together at right angles span the structural frame and create a two-way spanning floor system. The desire for transparency has been achieved by the large, open spaces on every level, and the full height sliding glass panels giving on to the terrace and second-floor balcony. The solid rear wall is used for the storage. The interior spaces are clear and unobstructed, and circulation and living areas almost merge. The landing or hall on the second floor is just punctuated by circular pods with overhead skylights, containing bath, dressing area and shower; they are like sculptural features in the open space.

Planners who give building permission are beginning to be more flexible in London, since the early eighties when modern architecture was seriously restricted, but it is still not common. Just as Michael Hopkins, whose highly regarded practice Romaniuk is an associate of, stood out among his generation for his own totally uncompromising house, so has Peter Romaniuk achieved a significant feat by building an utterly modern house in this urban context.

149

1. Section.

2. Axonometric study.

3. Third floor.

4. Second floor.

5. First floor.

6. Detail of the living room.

7. The kitchen is laid out around a free-standing bar.

8. Stairway leading to the bedrooms.

9. Detail of the washroom.

10. The sliding doors allow osmosis between the corridors and the bedrooms.

Kappe Tamuri Residence

Kappe Studio

LOCATION: TOPANGA, CALIFORNIA, U.S.A.

COMPLETION DATE: 1997.

ARCHITECTS: FINN KAPPE, MAUREEN TAMURI.

COLLABORATORS: REISS, BROWN, EKMEKJI;

WOODS ENGINEERING (STRUCTURAL),

RICHARD REISS (CIVIL), FINN KAPPE (LIGHTING),

FINN KAPPE (GENERAL CONTRACTOR).

PHOTOGRAPHERS: DAVID HEWITT/ANNE GARRISON ARCHITECTURAL

PHOTOGRAPHY.

This 3800 square foot house and studio was built on a downsloping 1.5 acre semi-rural site in the ruggedly beautiful Topanga Canyon area of Los Angeles County. The project was built as the Architects' family home and work place.

The main wing of the house is a large, two-story, shoebox-type space, a basic rectangular shape with operations from back to front to affect its spatial characteristics. This section of the house is oriented parallel to the slope of the land and seems to emerge from the hillside. Inside, the painted colors and materials are rich and warm reflecting tones of the surrounding canyon. The main social rooms are here in one continuous space overlaid in part by the main bedroom, study and catwalk. The kitchen is central and open, minimally defined by the island cabinet, lights and catwalk above. The dining table is situated opposite the kitchen. Again, subtle but clear use of the architecture reinforces the otherwise transparent room. Unquestionably, this is the most stunning room in the house. Somehow, Kappe and Tamuri have achieved a space which during the day, with its glass walls and high ceiling, seems to be outside, like a ledge on an exposed cliff; while at night the glass darkens and the redwood catwalk is lit from below shrinking and centering the room, making it an intimate camp in front of its fire.

The bedroom/studio wing is oriented parallel to the topography of the site and is anchored by a 10' wide lateral core situated between two block walls. The core consists of baths, laundry and mechanical room. The three zones of the solar assisted hydronic floor heating system eminate from this core. Laid against this 10' strip is the studio at grade level and the bedrooms above. All living spaces and even one of the baths open fluidly to decks and views which extend the interior spaces in ways that are hard to quantify.

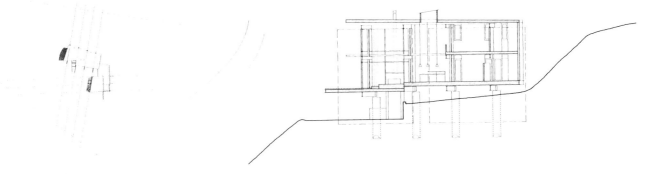

The resulting angle between the two wings of the house is 102.5 degrees. Like a piece of a walled city, this open L layout allows for and shelters a large courtyard in front of the house. As shown on the site plan, the formal layout of the house reflects a desire for the inclusion of the architecture within the larger landscape. And although Kappe likens the plan form to a truck and trailer about to jackknife, he also admits that the fanning characteristic of the straight lines of the plan may behave in a parabolic manner - implying curvature and softness which seems to hold resonance with the formation of the canyon itself.

Details were generated which expressed the inherent characteristics of each primary building material without straying far from its everyday usage. With careful combining, assemblage and construction (done by Kappe), it was hoped that the perception of these basic building materials might be transformed. For example, the concrete block walls were all identically scored horizontally to emphasize their gravity-based nature. The patterned spacing suggesting stone masonry or geotechnical strata. In addition, the walls were sandblasted and terminated at the same elevation to maintain similarity and modulation. However, their separation and differing orientation gives a sense of shifted release and even randomness.

As the house pivots to become parallel to the slope, it is lifted off the ground, hung between the rigid steel frames and the block walls. This helped to achieve a compact building footprint and minimized grading. Cool air storage for natural ventilation was also established under the shadow of the building. To the south and east are views of the largely unspoiled canyon lands. Here the solid and void characteristics of the block walls and glass walls were studied carefully to achieve simultaneous framing of interior spaces and exterior views.

1. The house rests on a sloping hillside.

2. Its L-shape means it is shut off from the roads which cross the site and open to views of less urban surroundings.

3,4. Nighttime views of the entrance.

5. Detail of the picture window.

6. First and second floors.

  1. Entrance.

  2. Living room.

  3. Kitchen.

  4. Dining room.

  5. Family room.

  6. Storage space.

  7. Study.

  8. Bedroom.

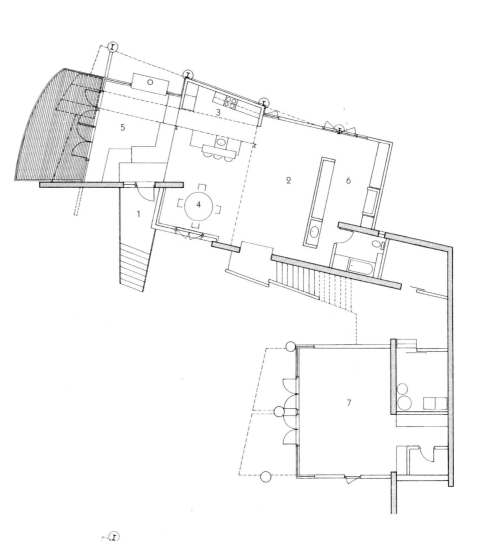

7. Several views of the living room.

8. One of the project's most judicious decisions was to separate the program out into several volumes. We started by simply seeking out a combination between the different structural parts to allow greater freedom in the interiors and in the flexibility of the walls." Finn Kappe

9. A narrow walkway leads from the master bedroom to a small balcony on the front facade.

10. The structure has been left bare throughout the house. Kappe combines laminated steel profiles with concrete block walls to close the space in.

7

8

9

Barnes House

Patkau Architects

Location: Nanaimo, British Columbia, Canada.

Completion date: 1993.

Architects: Tim Newton, John Patkau, Patricia Patkau, David Shone, Tom Robertson.

Collaborators: Fast & Epp Partners (structure), Robert Wall Ltd. (contractor).

Photographer: Undine Pröhl.

If your starting point is a site on Vancouver Island within a forested five acres, looking over the Strait of Georgia that divides the island from mainland Canada, many would ask how you could fail to create a beautiful home. Of course the resounding reply would be "in a million ways". Patkau Architects, fully aware of the natural beauty of British Columbia and its inevitable protagonism in the design, are also fully aware of the pitfalls. There is a simple beauty in this project that indicates that the thinking behind the design is very structured and studied. The architects' clarity of vision comes across in many ways: the luminous, fluid spaces, the fine details, the complex geometry of the timber roof.

The Vancouver-based architects confirm that the design of Barnes House is part of their current research based on three clear objectives: a search for the particular, a search for what is real and a search for heterogeneity. It is something of a reaction to post-modernism and the international bias of the modern movement.

The search for the particular as opposed to the general, is centered on the individual characteristics of the project: in this case it is the site, in its widest sense, including the whole region and figuratively speaking. The house is designed to enable its inhabitants to experience the place.

In their search for "the real", the architects consider the design should be based on what they are actually dealing with, not on some ideal. It is a more pragmatic approach. The topography of the site plays an important part. As Barnes House is built on an uneven, rocky outcrop, its structure is almost moulded to the land. It has an irregularity of form and variability of space and massing in common with the location. It nestles into the site, with the different levels

4

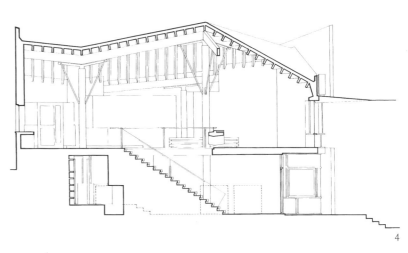

2

1

incorporated into its plan. Man makes concessions to nature, and not vice versa. Entry to the house is on the lower floor, housing studio and guest bedroom, through the striking "prow"; stairs lead to the main floor, making a sequence of movement which reinforces this relation to the site. Living room, dining room, kitchen and master bedroom are all in this large expansive space. Here, with the surrounding conifers and extensive views, there is a sense of being in the tree tops.

The heterogeneous nature of the house is inevitable after seeking out what is particular and what is real. Barnes House manifests it in formal/spatial terms: the conjunction of orthogonal and non-orthogonal geometries; the figural strength of the north and west elevations set against a figural weakness in the south and east elevations; the enormous timber beams in contrast to the slender, elegant steel.

The house is expressive in its construction, using basic materials on the whole. The shell is a conventional wood frame, stucco clad, on a reinforced-concrete grade beam foundation. Three concrete columns rise up through both floors to support the heavy roof. The steel, as a more refined, prefabricated material, is used for detailed, more decorative work like the stair rail, joints and the canopy over the huge window in the living room and the entrance below.

Barnes House is a far cry from the traditional Canadian log cabin, but the huge timbers and variety of attractive wood seem to provide some recognition of the fact this is logging territory. As a counterpoint the extensive use of glass, the minimalist window details and the bold use of concrete make it unmistakably contemporary.

3

1. The edges of the walls and
   the wedge-shaped
   profile in the picture
   window evoke the
   rugged topography
   of the place.

2. The architects purposely
   combine different materials:
   the metal-sheet canopy,
   wooden window frames
   and stuccoed outside walls.

3. Entrance stairway.

4. Section.

5. 6. Floor plans:

   1. Entrance.
   2. Studio.
   3. Bathroom.
   4. Guest room.
   5. Living room..
   6. Master bedroom.
   7. Dining room.
   8. Kitchen.
   9. Pantry.
   10. Terrace.
   11. Barbecue.
   12. Hollow for fire-lighting.

Following page:

7. General overview of the entrance
   via the upper floor, showing
   the dining room and kitchen.

8, 9, 10, 11, 12.
   Sequence of spaces on the
   upper floor.

13,14. Detail of the stairway.

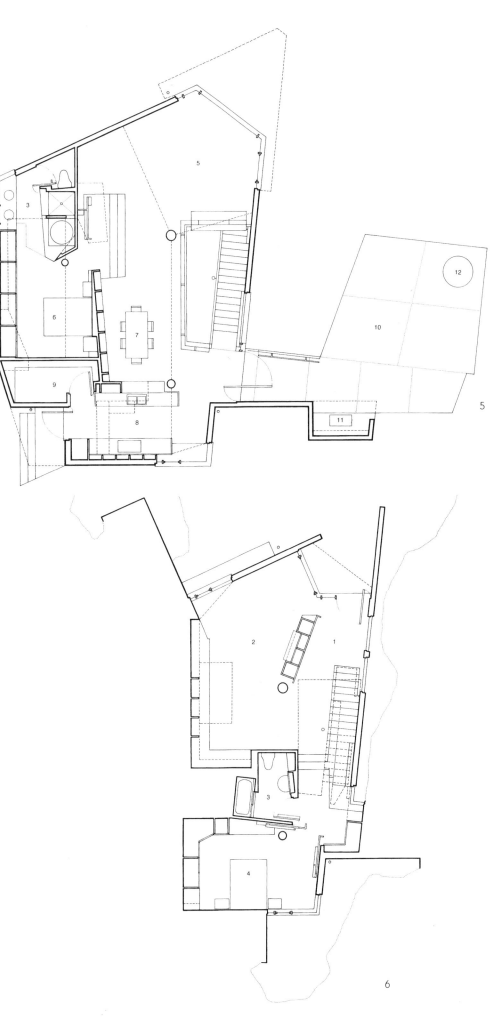

159

5

6

7

8

11

12

9

10

13

14

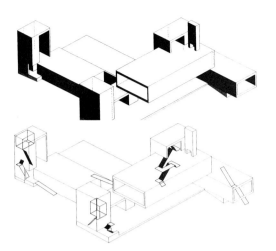

Type/Variant House

Vincent James

LOCATION: WISCONSIN, U.S.A.

DATE OF CONSTRUCTION: 1996.

ARCHITECTS: VINCENT JAMES, PAUL YAGGIE.

COLLABORATORS: NANCY BLANFARD, NATHAN KNUSTON, ANDREW DULL,
STEVE LAZEN, KRISTA SCHEIB, JULIE SNOW,
TAAVO SOMER, KATE WYBERG (DESIGN),
COEN + STUMPF AND ASSOCIATES (LANDSCAPE),
YERIGAN CONSTRUCTION (CONTRACTOR).

PHOTOGRAPHER: DON F. WONG.

The Type/Variant House is a 7,500 square foot building set in the North Woods. It has a monumental, academic air as if it were on a university campus.

The facthat architect Vincent James teaches at the University of Minnesota, and is known for his work on children's museums and other cultural buildings may have left its stamp. However the Type/Variant has been designed with a very different purpose: to be a lakeside summer home for a large family.

The fundamental idea behind the project actually came from James' clients who were fascinated by the concept of "Type/Variant". It can be interpreted as taking one "type" of object or being, and forming a collection of similar types, that are all slightly different from each other. The subtle differences between them create interesting relationships and as a composite whole they take on a different presence. The architect uses the analogy of a butterfly collection in a glass case: each one has an individual beauty, and the play between the similarities and differences gives the collection its aesthetic appeal.

Translated to the design of this home, the individual pieces are variations on the theme of a box. A series of wood-lined boxes, both horizontal and vertical, are placed orthogonally to each other and the house is derived from their composition. Even the outdoor spaces are designed within the same system. This design concept ties in with the client brief: a couple with five adult children wanting a vacation home for family gatherings:

1

2

3

4

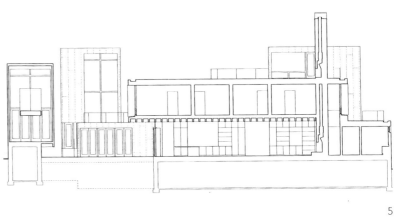

5

the individual members (with their own variants) can reunite here as one family.

Each space is allocated a size, shape and proportion according to its requirements both in mood and function; they respond to the rhythms and patterns of domestic life. Also the orientation and natural light is different in each space. The larger, living spaces and outdoor terraces on the upper floors are for communal activities, while the smaller spaces provide intimacy and solitude. The Douglas fir lining reinforces the quiet privacy in a comforting cave-like way, though it is not oppressive as the horizontal paneling guides the perspective outwards to the views through the window. There is even a space in total isolation for anyone who needs to break away (though still be linked to the group): a 24-foohigh guest tower is set apart to the south of the main building.

The architect was anxious not to mimic the traditional rustic buildings that are the pride of the Upper Midwest, and treasured by the people from Chicago and the Twin Cities (St Paul and Minneapolis) who flock to this dramatically beautiful area for vacations. James sought inspiration in the more industrial buildings in the area, like granaries, valuing the "clear, straightforward quality to their construction" which comes from the direct relationship between their use and form. This also suited the clients who were keen to avoid rustic sentimentalism. The industrial edge is counterbalanced though by the warmth of the materials used: Douglas fir and bluestone are predominant in the interiors and the exterior walls are copper clad. These three are assembled in a variety of rhythmic patterns.

A key element in the design concept is the effect of time and weathering on the materials; the house will evolve over the years. The copper will change from its original pinkish - orange to blue and purple, a deep brown and then the bright green of verdigris. These subtle changes and the different shades of the bluestone harmonize with the textures, colors and seasonal changes in the natural surroundings. This striking Modernist house is by no means one of a type, but in its own particular way will grow and become an integral part of the North Woods.

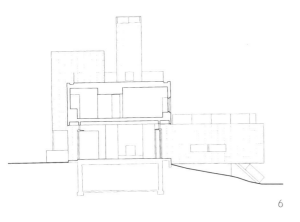

1. The copper facades
   are meant to change
   with the passage of time.

2. The house is raised up
   on a slate base.

3. Detail of the entrance
   to the inner court.

4. There are many semi-closed
   outdoor spaces between
   the various volumes.

5. Longitudinal section
   looking west.

6. Cross section looking north.

7 , 8. Two images of the inner
   courtyard where the firewood
   is kept.

9. Interior of the living room.

7

8

9

10. Almost all the interior is
    wood-lined.

11. Stairway leading up to the bedrooms.

12. First floor.

13. Second floor.

14. Third floor.

15. The owners wanted welcoming,
    comfortable interiors.

166

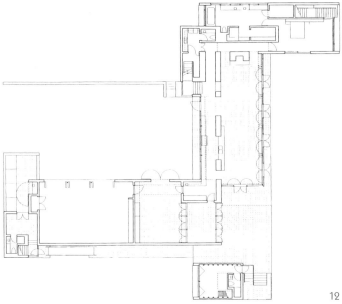

12

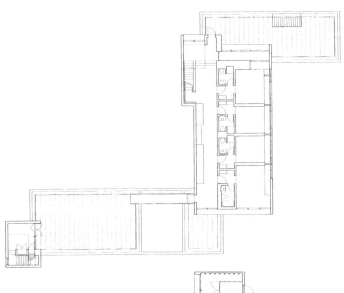

13

10

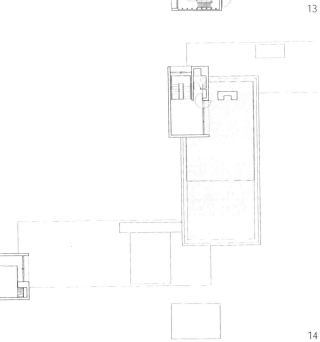

11

14

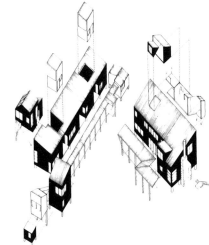

Collective Housing for the Cheesecake Consortium

Fernau & Hartman

LOCATION: MENDOCINO COUNTY, CALIFORNIA, U.S.A.

COMPLETION DATE: 1994.

ARCHITECTS: RICHARD FERNAU, LAURA HARTMAN, DAVID KAU.

COLLABORATORS: TIM GRAY, KIMBERLY MOSES,
EMILY STUSSI (TEAM PROJECT),
DENNIS McCROSKEY (STRUCTURE),
WILLIAM MAH ENGINEERS (MECHANICAL),
ZIEGER ENGINEERS (ELECTRICITY),
JIM BOUDOURES (CONTRACTOR).

PHOTOGRAPHER: RICHARD BARNES.

It may not be everybody's idea of Shangri-La, but as an exercise in co-habitation and confronting the euphemistically-coined "Golden years", the "Cheesecake Consortium" is innovative, challenging and very admirable. As an architectural exercise it also represented a challenge for the Berkeley firm Fernau and Hartman, on many levels: from coping with eleven individuals as The Client to working within quite a modest budget. Happily a great deal of determination and goodwill on both sides helped the project to run smoothly and successfully, as several awards prove. One from the California branch of the A.I.A. described it as "a socially innovative, environmentally responsible and financially viable alternative for community living".

The idea behind the project was to build collective housing for a group of friends (4 couples and 3 singles), to be able to live together and give each other mutual support in the latter years of their lives. Currently in the forties to sixties age bracket, their friendships go back a long way and have been thoroughly tested. Most of them still work and live elsewhere but plan to retire here. Set in a 13-acre site in Mendocino County, north of San Francisco, the Cheesecake compound is built on a flat shelf in the 100-year-old flood plain of the Navarro River in the midst of a redwood forest. The apparently whimsical name actually belongs to the site: the previous owners were an Italian family named Casatas, loosely translated as "cheese pie" and adopted by the local community as "cheesecake".

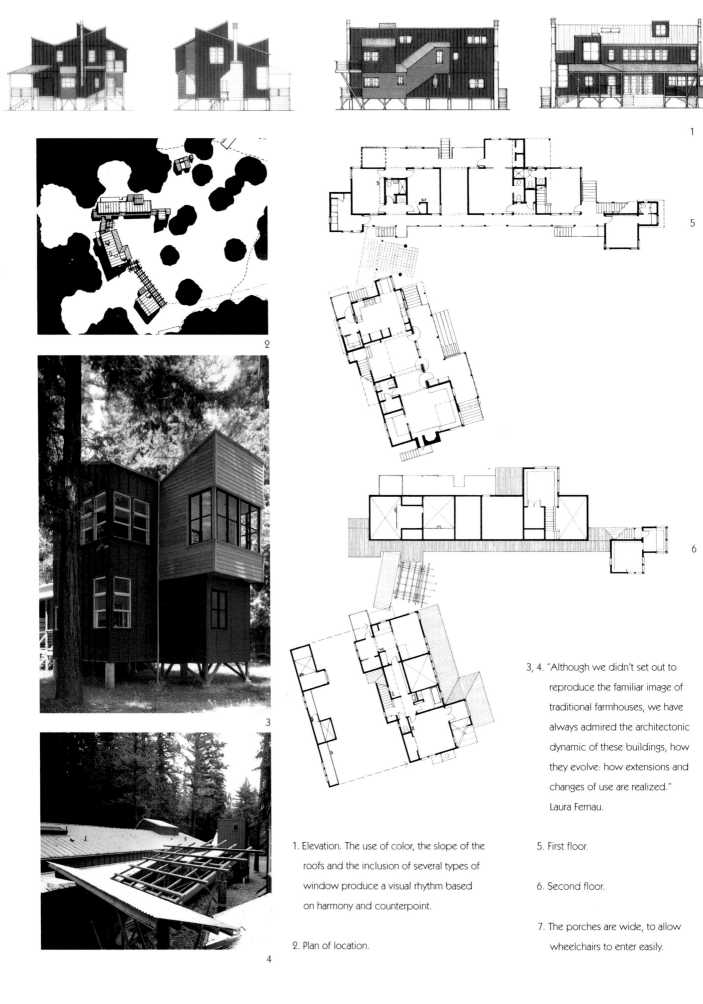

1

2

3

5

6

4

3, 4. "Although we didn't set out to
reproduce the familiar image of
traditional farmhouses, we have
always admired the architectonic
dynamic of these buildings, how
they evolve: how extensions and
changes of use are realized."
Laura Fernau.

1. Elevation. The use of color, the slope of the
roofs and the inclusion of several types of
window produce a visual rhythm based
on harmony and counterpoint.

2. Plan of location.

5. First floor.

6. Second floor.

7. The porches are wide, to allow
wheelchairs to enter easily.

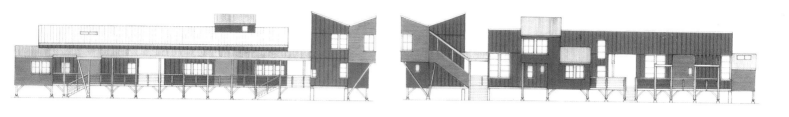

8. The clients wanted big interiors to hold family get-togethers.

9. The four trees which were felled to build the houses were used for the interiors, the pergolas and the furnishings.

10. Kitchen detail.

9

10

Architects Richard Fernau and Laura Hartman are known for their imaginative, environmentally respectful projects and collaborative approach and for their keen interest in social issues. "We loved the idea of doing housing for a group. This was a project with modest financial parameters, and we welcomed the cost challenges." In turn they were impressed by the attitude of the group who were easier to deal with than a single client; decisions were democratic but kept tight and organized.

The compound has a youthful feel about it in appearance and spirit, like a camp or new settlement. Ironic, considering its purpose, but a true reflection of the energy behind it. There are communal rooms for sundry activities and the partners plan to spend time hiking in the surrounding forests and playing volleyball. Nevertheless they are realistic about the future so the design includes such pragmatic details as 34-inch- wide doors for wheel chairs, space for ramps and an elevator. A thoughtful detail is the alternation of public and private spaces – for example to reach the laundry or library one passes the individual living quarters – which creates social circulation, avoiding any risk of one member becoming isolated.

There are three main buildings, raised five feet from the ground because of the flood plain, a bath house, a pool and tent platform and, in a separate clearing, a garden. The three main ones are the workshop, the lodge – housing communal kitchen, living room, dining room and office – and a bedroom wing that incorporates a library and laundry/sewing room. Interior space is over 5,000 square feet and exterior space in the form of verandas, a dog trot, tent decks and a pavilion total 3,000 square feet. Aware of the farm building ethic, but anxious not to fall into the picturesque, the architects designed a simple, inexpensive construction: a wood frame on concrete piers, with sidings of painted plywood and battens, stained cedar and painted corrugated metal. The roof is painted panel and unpainted corrugated metal. Where possible recycled materials were used: wood milled from the trees cleared on the site was used for the decking, banisters and dining table.

The communal spaces are all subtly designed to cope with large influxes of this enormous extended family (26 children and 9 grandchildren –to date...). Rooms spill out onto wide porches, guests can sleep on the tent platforms, or in the "dog-trot" wing (named after the southern tradition of roofed passages between structures). There is little likelihood of being neglected by your family here in this attractive and welcoming corner of Northern California. It is the antithesis of the conventional retirement home and the visitors will keep coming.

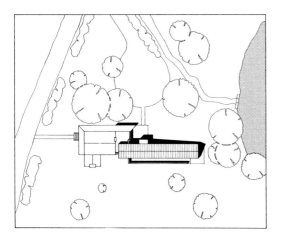

Linear House

Peter Gluck

LOCATION: MILLERTON, NEW YORK, U.S.A.

DATE OF CONSTRUCTION: 1996.

ARCHITECT: PETER GLUCK.

COLLABORATORS: SUKI DIXON (PROJECT MANAGER).

PHOTOGRAPHER: PAUL WARCHOL.

Just as many farmhouses have become purely domestic homes rather than working farms, so has the relationship of their occupants with the natural surroundings evolved. They see it as an object of leisure and contemplation rather than a source of income or survival. Farmers have always had a pragmatic attitude, and as in this early nineteenth-century farmhouse in Millerton, New York, it was typical to build the house right on the road for better access to the market towns. Similarly, there was none of the contemporary interest in linking the interior of the home with the exterior – indoor life would be more inward-looking and focused on the kitchen range. In this case there was no seeking out the nearby pond, waterfall and apple orchard, which were both invisible and inaccessible.

With a brief to extend this farmhouse for a family of four with growing children, New York architect Peter Gluck's approach was to re-establish the house's relationship with its environment. His late twentieth-century solutions counterbalanced the early nineteenth-century shortcomings. The eighty-foot extension stretches away from the existing house, turning its back on the road and getting deeper into the countryside. It also connects the home directly with the landscape by following the natural slope and arriving at the pond area: the way the building resolves the change in level in its course to eventually become single storey is gracefully handled. Also an exterior walkway on the upper level makes it possible to walk from the original house to the pond.

The new wing is a pure linear shape, in bold contrast to the old farmhouse with its tacked-on parts. Its ninety-foot metal shed roof encloses the whole program, unifying the composition and allowing changes in the form below it not to interfere with the overall control

1. The slope of the ground sees the
   new module sink down as it moves
   away from the existing house.

2. The different treatment given to the new
   roof shows Gluck's field of intervention.

3. The meeting point of the two constructions
   is the stairway.

4. Front elevation.

5. Section.

of the composition. Though the difference is striking, the simple geometry and strong lines seem to complement the old house, and the extension is reminiscent of traditional farm outbuildings. The new roof overlaps at either end covering a terrace on the upper level of the old house and forming a covered porch at its end. This reinforces the esthetics of haylofts and barns.

The difficult problem of linking old and new is resolved with the construction of a single-story link, which is used as a transition area. The new extension can then be an uncompromised single volume, like the original house. A new kitchen has been built in this space so that the two buildings are united in day-to-day living terms. However the two roofs are separate: the gap between the gable end of each marks the division of old and new, and at the same time sets up a relationship between them; furthermore one of the tall timber posts supporting the new gable comes down outside the single-story volume, creating a subtle interlocking effect.

The structural rationale behind the design is a series of eightbays giving a flexibility of room sizes, openings and enclousures. The rooms occupy the entire 14-foot width of the extension. Within this simple geometry different rooms have been created – a studio, master bedroom and children's room. This building has a more industrial, larger, tougher feel about it with its steel staircase, metal roof and chimneys and larger panes of glass: a reflection of technological advances since the nineteenth century as well as the changing demands of the inhabitants.

Linear House is a classic example of the "contextual modernism" practised by Peter Gluck. As in similar projects of his, he has managed to create something contemporary which is at the same time sensitive to the original and to its setting, a building that complements it without imitating or overshadowing it.

2

3

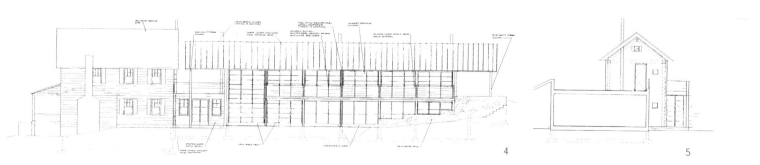

4   5

6. Plan of the stairway.

7. Studio on the first floor.

8. First floor.

9. Second floor.

10. The foyer is paved with slate, whereas the
stairway is constructed out of metal.

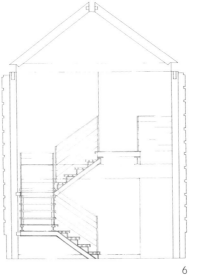

6

7

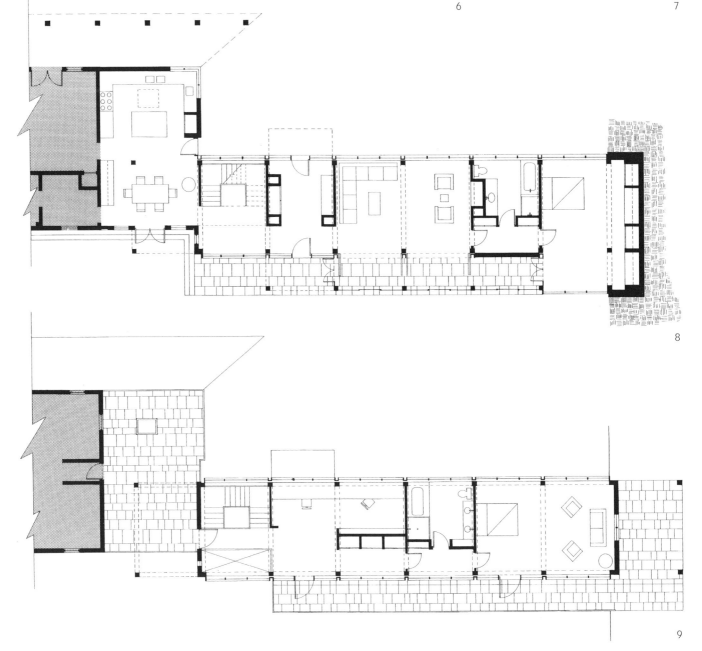

8

9

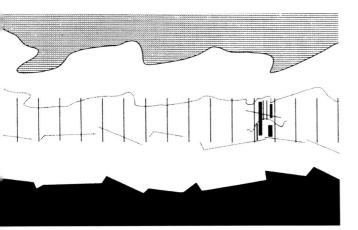

Capistrano Beach House

Rob Wellington Quigley

LOCATION: CAPISTRANO BEACH, CALIFORNIA, USA.

COMPLETION DATE: 1994.

ARCHITECT: ROB WELLINGTON QUIGLEY.

COLLABORATORS: TEDDY CRUZ, CATHERINE HERBST (DESIGN TEAM),
INTEGRATED STRUCTURAL DESIGN
(STRUCTURAL CONSULTANTS),
MARK FALCANE (GENERAL CONTRATOR).

PHOTOGRAPHER: UNDINE PRÖHL.

The elongated plot is on a narrow strip of land, merging with the sand to the west, and with a backdrop of high, windswept cliffs to the east. This context is mirrored in the design and in the materials used: the east/west-oriented architectural planes reinforce the rigid, parallel property lines while the north/south elements are more evocative of the surrounding natural forces, the effect of the sea and the wind on the shore and cliffs echoed in gentle curves and eroded, sculptural shapes.

This 3,700 square-foot house has all the apparent glamour of the California Dream: large expanses of glass over looking the Pacific Ocean, wooden decks jutting into the dazzling white sand, shady upper decks to enjoy the sea breezes in privacy, a virgin beach for early morning exercise. But under the sound guidance of Rob Quigley, with the "remarkable energy and ethicality that make him the signal architect he is today", there is no chance of it falling into such a clichéd category.

Quigley's designs have always been true to the reality they are in contextually, culturally and climatically. The dramatic and exciting contrasts between the ocean and the land are interpreted architecturally: thick walls of poured concrete set off glass pavilions; deep shade and dappled light are contrasted against the dazzling glare of the sand; exposed, extrovert decks and terraces as opposed to quiet, private areas.

Circulation through the house is also full of contrasts in both the interior and exterior. Entrance on the east side is through two iron gates which lead to an intimate, formal vegetable garden enclosed by 6 feet-high glass walls. A concrete "pier" crosses the sand to the porch and front door which face the cliffs and look on to the court-yard garden, perhaps the only "suburban" element in the whole design. The hall follows the curved glass wall and opens dramatically into the spacious living room, with its exposed roof beams and expansive view of the ocean. Along the beach side of the house is a small sitting room shaded by lattice work and a low-ceilinged dining room, both providing more private areas from the living room which through its mahogany and glass doors is almost part of the beach.

2

183

In his bid to design authentically Californian architecture, the choice of materials has always been a key issue for Quigley. The stucco and concrete vernacular of early twentieth-century Californian architects, like his mentor Irving Gill, has become his trademark. Here, the two-story structure consists of a poured-in-place concrete spine with cantilevered concrete floor slabs. A traditional wood frame clad in black asphalt shingles is used for the bedroom wing. Two guest bedroom suites above the garage are fronted by an asp-halt shingle screen. The exposed concrete provides attractive sculp-tural and geometric shapes both inside and outside: a majestic set-ting for the fireplace, different levels and walkways in the sand, the striking deco-like concrete spine and so on. As a counter balance to the expanses of concrete and glass, a series of redwood lattice structures, stained grey, are used for cladding or for shade and pri-vacy. Reminiscent of original beach huts, they are just one of the many elements that make this elegant Beach House a truly Californian building.

3

4

1. View from the street.

2. Facade overlooking the beach.

3,4. The porch and terraces allow the
    house to appropriate the beach.

5. Detail of the central garden.

5

6. First floor.

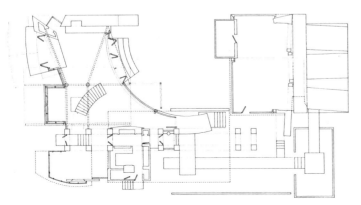

7. Second floor.

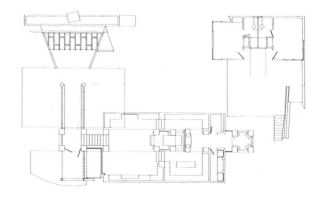

House in Tateshina

Yoshihiko Iida

Location: Tateshina, Nagano, Japan.

Completion date: 1994.

Architect: Yoshihiko Iida.

Collaborator: Niitsu (constructor)

Photographer: Koumei Tanaka.

The house is located in a resort area at the foot of Mount Tateshina in Nagano. The terrain slopes gently towards the southwest, and a forest surrounds the house.

As Iida himself explains, a vacation home is not subject to the same hierarchies as a first residence. The relationships between members are more relaxed. Different activities can often take place in the same place, since they do not require as much isolation and concentration. Finally there is generally a closer relationship with nature, since vacationers usually want to enjoy life in the outdoors. For this reason, many of the most innovative and compelling architectural works take the form in this type of homes, since the owners' needs and desires require more open spaces with a less conventional layout.

Iida's project takes shape from a basic design consisting of two rectangular volumes, arranged parallel to one another, but slightly displaced. Both are located along the slope of the land, and access is provided at the highest point. Starting from the vestibule, a ramp descends along the natural slope of the hill, leading the visitor to the living room and the large wooden patio at the other end of the house. The ramp then continues until it fades into the forest.

A second ramp leads up from the vestibule to the neighboring building. On the first floor is the bathroom, an unusually open room with panoramic views of the forest, the perfect spot to relax for hours in

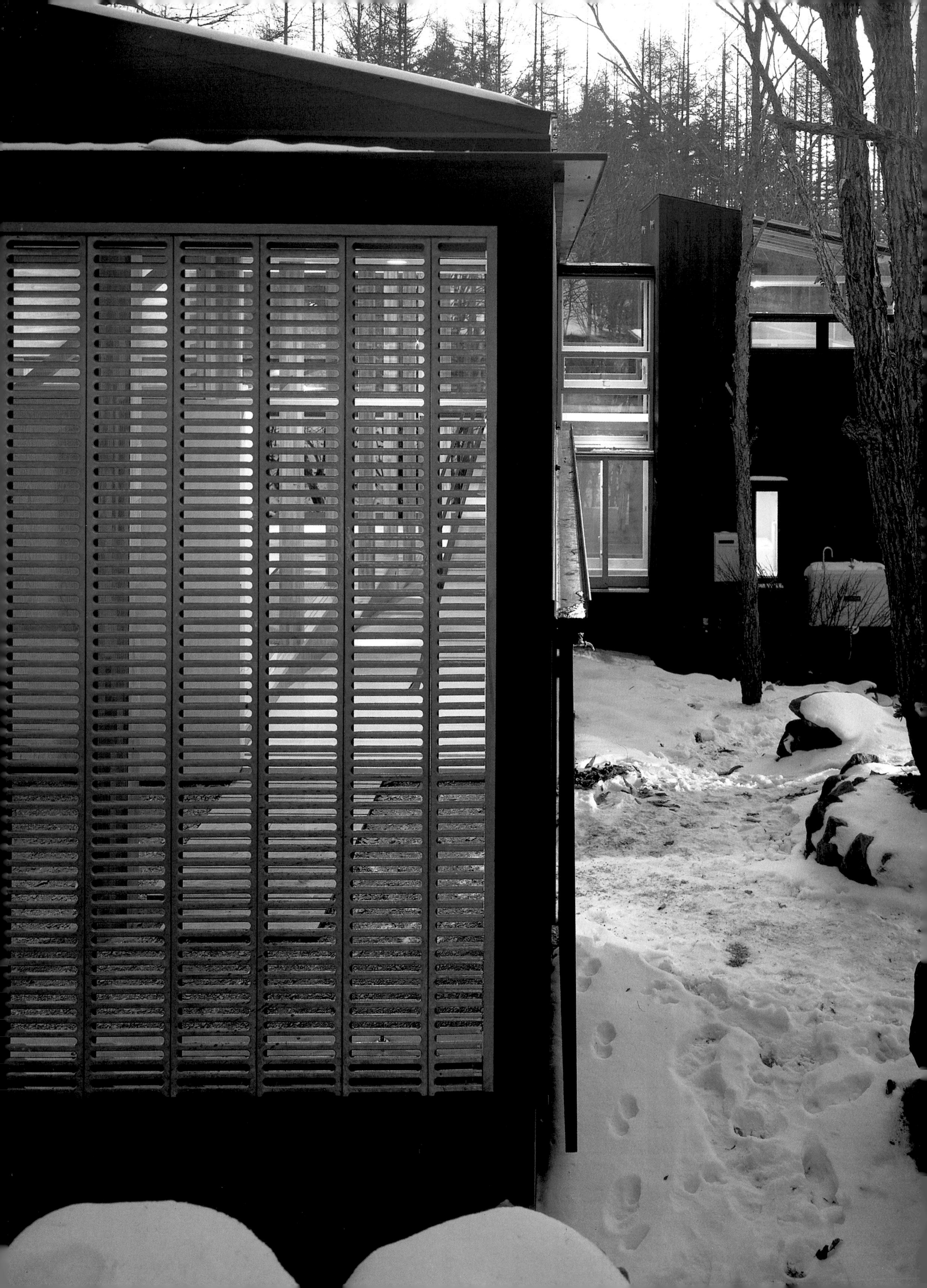

the bathtub. An exterior staircase leads from the contiguous patio to the wooden platform on the ground floor.

In this way, the house is arranged around a circular route which links the two floors and the interior to the patios. As in Iida's other project included in this book, the "O" Residence, the itinerary around the house is the axis of the house which determines the distribution and design of the other spaces.

Architecture can ignore time and be constructed from fixed, independent images. This is only possible, however, when it takes into account the pace, pauses, speed and itineraries of its inhabitants. It is only then that it transcends constructive logic, functional arrangement of rooms, and the purely visual and physical attributes of its volumes and becomes a harmonious construction which invites the person who inhabits it to experience space in a richer, more complete, less arbitrary way.

In the largest room, which holds the vestibule, tatami room, dining room and living room, the various spaces are terraced according to the slope of the terrain and the ramp. It is in effect one large double-height room, with closed side walls, open at the front and back. At each end, a patio connects the interior with the forest.

Seen in this light, Yoshihiko Iida's project might be considered to be the simplest construction possible: little more than a couple of walls and a roof placed along one of the paths that cross the mountain with, at the side of the path, a modest refuge for sleeping and washing.

1. First floor.

2. Second floor.

3. View of the dining room.

4. The whole interior is wood lined.

5. A shoji screen separates the tatami room.

6. The itinerary through the house creates a pause in our route through the wood.

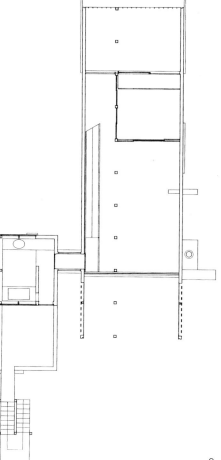

1

2

3

4

5

6